THE COMMERCIAL BAR ASSOCIATION (COMBAR) 1989–2014

In 2014 the Commercial Bar Association celebrated its 25th anniversary. When Lord Mackay's Green Papers, and especially that on 'The Work and Organisation of the Legal Profession', were published, the survival of the Bar was brought into question, and this was the catalyst for the formation of COMBAR. Since then, it has gone from strength to strength.

This volume is a collection of contributions from a number of different people who have been involved with COMBAR over the years. It includes texts from senior judiciary, past chairs, honorary overseas members, VIP annual lectures and lectures from guest speakers, amusing anecdotes and much more.

The Commercial Bar Association (COMBAR) 1989–2014

Celebrating the First 25 Years

Edited by
Stephen Moriarty QC

· HART ·
PUBLISHING
OXFORD AND PORTLAND, OREGON
2016

Published in the United Kingdom by Hart Publishing Ltd
16C Worcester Place, Oxford, OX1 2JW
Telephone: +44 (0)1865 517530
Fax: +44 (0)1865 510710
E-mail: mail@hartpub.co.uk
Website: http://www.hartpub.co.uk

Published in North America (US and Canada) by
Hart Publishing
c/o International Specialized Book Services
920 NE 58th Avenue, Suite 300
Portland, OR 97213-3786
USA
Tel: +1 503 287 3093 or toll-free: (1) 800 944 6190
Fax: +1 503 280 8832
E-mail: orders@isbs.com
Website: http://www.isbs.com

Hart Publishing is an imprint of Bloomsbury Publishing plc.

British Library Cataloguing in Publication Data
Data Available

Library of Congress Cataloging-in-Publication Data

Names: Moriarty, Stephen, editor. | Commercial Bar Association (Great Britain), honouree.

Title: The Commercial Bar Association (COMBAR) 1989–2014 : celebrating the first 25 years / Edited by Stephen Moriarty.

Description: Portland, Oregon : Hart Publishing, 2016. | Includes bibliographical references.

Identifiers: LCCN 2015039913 | ISBN 9781849467056 (hardback : alk. paper)

Subjects: LCSH: Commercial Bar Association (Great Britain) | Bar associations—Great Britain.

Classification: LCC KD456.C66 C66 2016 | DDC 340.06/041—dc23 LC record available at http://lccn.loc.gov/2015039913

ISBN: 978-1-84946-705-6

Typeset by Compuscript Ltd, Shannon
Printed and bound in Great Britain by
Lightning Source UK Ltd

Foreword

In 2014, the Commercial Bar Association (COMBAR) celebrated its 25th anniversary. Joe Smouha QC, COMBAR's then Chairman, asked me to chair a small committee to decide upon a number of initiatives to mark this important occasion. In keeping with the convivial spirit which marks COMBAR's annual North American meeting, and in particular the annual dinner at that event, one thing we most certainly wanted to do was hold a grand gala 25th birthday dinner in London. That dinner took place in the summer of last year in the splendid setting of Drapers' Hall, and it was marvellous to see the dinner so well-attended, not just by the UK members of COMBAR and our English commercial judges, but also by so many of our Honorary Overseas Members who came directly to London from the annual North American meeting in Seville, before travelling home to various destinations around the globe.

The second thing we decided upon, in the interests of encouraging greater diversity at the Commercial Bar, was to establish a scholarship scheme enabling young people from a broader range of backgrounds to spend time in barristers' chambers, and see what life at the Commercial Bar entails. That scheme is now up and running, and the first beneficiaries spent time in various sets of chambers last month. It was a great success, and I hope COMBAR will continue to support this scheme in the coming years.

This book is the product of the third initiative we decided upon. It consists of a miscellany of chapters/papers—some legal and some non-legal; some serious and some light-hearted; some already published elsewhere, some specially written for this book—but all of which are COMBAR/Commercial Bar-related. I hope readers will enjoy dipping into this miscellany, and will get a real sense of the sheer variety of interests which combine to make COMBAR what it has become over the past 25 years.

I would like to thank all the contributors to this book for generously agreeing to participate in the venture, and also Lucy Colter (Chair of Junior COMBAR) for having dutifully checked all the contributions, eradicating a number of inconsistencies and typographical errors. As always, thanks are also due to COMBAR's administrator, Veronica Kendall. Without her patient chiding, this book celebrating COMBAR's first 25 years would quite possibly not have found its way to the publishers until COMBAR was on the eve of its 50th birthday. Having now got this book out of the way, I very much look forward to seeing that companion volume in due course.

Stephen Moriarty QC
Editor
August 2015

Former Chairs of COMBAR

Six of its former Chairmen have gone on to become Judges of the Commercial Court. Thus, COMBAR truly represents the whole Commercial Bar and constitutes a body of specialist expertise and advocacy skills in banking, insurance, international trade, shipping, aviation and other key commercial activities.

1989–1991	Sir David Steel (now retired from the Commercial Court) Honorary Member of COMBAR
1991–1992	Sir Anthony Colman (now retired from the Commercial Court) Honorary Member of COMBAR
1992–1993	Sir Bernard Rix (now retired from the Court of Appeal)
1993–1995	Christopher Clarke QC (now the Rt Hon Lord Justice Christopher Clarke)
1995–1997	John Jarvis QC
1997–1999	Ian Glick QC
1999–2001	Barbara Dohmann QC
2001–2003	Michael Brindle QC
2003–2005	William Blair QC (now the Hon Mr Justice Blair)
2005–2007	Robin Knowles CBE QC (now the Hon Mr Justice Knowles CBE, QC)
2007–2009	Ali Malek QC
2009–2011	Christopher Hancock QC
2011–2013	Stephen Moriarty QC
2013–2015	Joe Smouha QC
2015–	Laurence Rabinowitz QC

Contents

1

COMBAR History

SIR DAVID STEEL (CHAIRMAN, 1989 TO 1991)

IT IS DIFFICULT after 25 years to recapture the circumstances giving rise to the birth of COMBAR. There was a feeling of legal revolution in the air. The Thatcher administration had turned its attention to what was perceived as the last of the professional cartels, needing root and branch reform. There had been earlier inquiries—the Benson Commission (1979) report had offered no significant changes, and the Marre Committee (1988) report was hopelessly divided. But in the meantime the Farrand Committee (1984) report had led to the loss by solicitors of their conveyancing monopoly. One reaction of the Law Society had been to press for the abolition of the barristers' monopoly on right of audience.

The Conservative government published three Green Papers in January 1989. The major proposal in regard to rights of audience was that whilst both solicitors and barristers would be qualified to practise in the lower courts, they would all require a certificate of competence to work in the higher courts. Many of us were greatly concerned about a system of licensing to appear in the higher courts, which were in effect the only courts in which commercial barristers practised from the outset.

These concerns added to earlier unease about a number of matters. First the Commercial Bar, despite being a uniquely specialised group, with its own judges and court, had no representative body. It sat rather uncomfortably under the umbrella of the London Common Law Bar Association, which was far too large and disparate a body to properly represent the interest of the Commercial Bar. Second, many within the Commercial Bar (and its judges) were already pressing for improvements in court facilities, an ambition which it was perceived had a chance only if there was strong cohesive pressure from the Commercial Bar as a whole. Third, the profession was increasingly opening up the opportunities for direct access. With the Commercial Bar's special position as acting, if not exclusively at least largely for foreign clients, it was clearly advantageous to ensure that the potential for direct access became widely known abroad. Last, it was also becoming increasingly apparent that the Commercial Bar needed to divert more of its time and resources to ensure proper post-qualification training and a marked improvement in pupillage facilities.

A White Paper was published in July 1989, but in the meantime COMBAR had been formed. Whilst the White Paper was high on the agenda of the newly formed association, various organisational decisions taken at an early stage were pivotal in achieving success:

a) Recruiting membership primarily on a chambers basis. This ensured a 'corporate' interest.
b) Appointing a secretariat. This was a first for a Bar association. The first Secretary was Marion Hollidge, and we owe a great deal of gratitude for all her initial work.
c) Publication of a brochure. Again this was a most effective marketing tool, both at home and overseas, to which all members could contribute.
d) Creation of liaison committees. Initially this was for the US and for the EU. Their continuation over a quarter century with many of the original overseas members continuing to attend is a matter of great satisfaction.

These foundation stones of COMBAR have proved both enduring and worthwhile. In the result, COMBAR became and has remained the most influential and successful of the Bar associations. This is reflected in the fact that the association attracted almost all practitioners at the Commercial Bar to join from the outset. When its formation was announced in August 1989, it already had 450 members from 21 sets of chambers.

Being the first chairman of COMBAR (with Tony Colman as my deputy) was not just a great honour but a very rewarding experience. It is a matter of considerable satisfaction that it has gone from strength to strength ever since.

2

The Origins of the British in Virginia

SIR ANTHONY COLMAN

In April 2007, COMBAR held its North American meeting in Richmond, Virginia, in conjunction with the Rule of Law Conference to celebrate the common law 400 years after the founding of the first permanent settlement in America at Jamestown.

Sir Anthony Colman (now retired) was a guest judge at the meeting, and together with Sir David Steel, both gave lunchtime talks in Richmond to COMBAR delegates. Sir Anthony Colman practised as a barrister of Gray's Inn at the Commercial Bar from 1962 to 1992 and specialised in primary insurance and reinsurance including marine insurance, maritime disputes, banking and international trade and distributorship agreements, ICC and ICSID arbitrations, including acting as ICC, LCIA and ICSID arbitrator. He was the Chairman of the Commercial Bar Association (COMBAR) from 1991–92.

It is as always a great honour and pleasure to be invited to take part in the annual meeting of COMBAR's North American Committee.

It is a particular pleasure to find here today David Steel, who was the first Chairman of COMBAR immediately before I took over, as well as Bill Blair—a very early committee member and later Chairman. It is also a great pleasure to see two of the original members of the North American Liaison Committee, which I suggested should be formed at a meeting on 13 November 1989. Those two are our loyal supporters—John Lorn McDougall from Toronto, and Steve Rosenfeld from New York. It is wonderfully rewarding to see how strong the North American membership has now become. It has grown in strength with COMBAR itself. The latter now has some 1100 members.

But today I am not going to dwell on the origins of COMBAR in North America but rather on the origins of the British in Virginia. I want to talk in particular about the one man whose obsessive drive and determination led directly to the Jamestown Declaration—Sir Walter Raleigh. And, as this meeting runs parallel to that of the American Inns of Court on the Rule of Law, I want to dwell on the supreme irony that it was Raleigh who was brought to his end by what we here would now regard as a total travesty of the Rule of Law.

As I shall explain later, it is quite a coincidence which makes it possible for me to tell you what follows.

By 1584 Raleigh had become Queen Elizabeth's favourite. She, in her late 40s, had grown quite passionate about him, who was about 30, and she bestowed great wealth on him, as well as the monopoly for the exploration and plantation by way of settlement of the southern part of North America. He was determined to establish a settlement there but equally determined to plan this operation with extreme care and on the basis of exhaustive scientific research. Elizabeth had given him a lease of Durham House, an old building of Norman origin, which stood where Embankment Gardens now are, alongside the River Thames, just east of Embankment Underground Station. There, he set up a planning headquarters covering navigation and North American geography, including climate and vegetation. He appointed as advisers the brilliant Oxford mathematician, Harriott, and the navigational expert, Hakluyt. In 1584 he sent a reconnaissance expedition which located Roanoke as a suitable site for a settlement. This was an island located within the Outer Banks, not far from where Jamestown was eventually to be founded. The expedition returned to England with two Indians who were duly installed at Durham House so as to enable the local Indian language, Algonkian, to be studied and phoneticised.

Elizabeth refused to put up any money for the settlement. She did however provide one of her own ships, the *Tiger*, together with four hundred pounds' worth of gunpowder; and she contributed her own very special idea, namely, the title for the whole territory which, after all, was to belong to her eventually, and was to be Virginia. She appointed Raleigh as controller of the enterprise and knighted him at the beginning of 1585. The expedition to Virginia was planned as the biggest settlement expedition ever undertaken from England. It was financed by the City of London merchants who bought shares in the product of one summer season's privateering against such Spanish vessels as the fleet could capture without going off-route!

The destination was to be Roanoke. This small island, just south of the eventual site of Jamestown, was a hopeless location. It was already overcrowded with Indians and had very little land which was cultivatable, as well as being plagued with mosquitoes.

The expedition was something of a disaster. The *Tiger*, on which practically all the perishable supplies had been loaded, ran aground not far from Roanoke and punctured her hull. Much of the supplies, including vital foodstuffs, animals and grain seed, were lost. After the settlers eventually landed, it was realised they did not have enough supplies to support all the settlers through the on-coming winter. In the result, only 107 were left at Roanoke and the rest were taken back to England. As it happened, there was not enough food even to support those who remained, and there were too many gentry in the party who were neither willing nor able to hunt or fish or cultivate the land. Worse still, as the food situation and the general conditions deteriorated, they all fell out with each other.

After a very, very hard winter, during which the settlers were dependent on buying what little food they could get from the Indians, Raleigh had sent out a relieving party with further supplies. However, Sir Francis Drake, who was on his way back from having sacked the Spanish settlement at Santo Domingo in Hispaniola, arrived at Roanoke with a fleet of some 23 ships, rescued most of the surviving settlers and took them home. Amongst them was Harriott, who brought back samples of wild tobacco from Roanoke, and he and Raleigh then promoted the use of tobacco at Court, ostensibly for medicinal purposes, so initiating what became a very widespread habit in the next few years. It was a typical misfortune that Raleigh's supply boat which was sent out to Roanoke arrived only three days after all the settlers had already left with Sir Francis Drake.

In 1587 Raleigh sent another expedition to Virginia under John White, the artist, not to Roanoke but to Chesapeake Bay. This time women were sent out as members of the party. White, brilliant artist though he was (his pictures are currently part of an excellent exhibition in London), was totally lacking in leadership qualities. Unfortunately, and with typical misfortune, so far as Raleigh was concerned, the leading Captain of the expedition, Juan Fernandez, mutinied and refused to take the settlers to Chesapeake Bay and insisted—contrary to his orders—on landing them all at Roanoke. The settlers then deposed White as leader and forced him to return to England, 112 of them remaining on Roanoke.

Raleigh's plans for stabilising the settlement were then completely scuppered by war with Spain and the advent of the Armada, and it was not until 1590 that he could send another expedition, again under White, back to Roanoke to discover the fate of the 112 settlers. He arrived there in March 1590 to find the place completely deserted, a message having been carved into one of the trees indicating that the settlers had gone to another island, which was part of the Outer Banks. But the expedition gave up the search without finding any of them.

Raleigh then made a fatal mistake. He secretly married and had a child with one of Queen Elizabeth's ladies in waiting, Bess Throckmorton, without first obtaining Elizabeth's consent. When in 1592 she discovered what had happened, both of them were thrown into the Tower of London. They were, however, released on Sir Robert Cecil's advice about five weeks later, but it was then too late for Raleigh to regain the favours of Elizabeth, who in the meantime had become much taken with Robert Devereux, Earl of Essex.

By this time Raleigh was very short of money and still in disgrace. In 1595, mindful that his monopoly of settlement and exploitation of Virginia would be lost unless he could establish continuity of settlement there, he mounted an expedition to Guiana in search of the fabled gold mine at El Dorado in order to replenish his finances and also for the purpose, on the way home, of receiving or rescuing the settlers who had been left at Roanoke in 1587. Misfortune stalked him yet again. He completely failed to find any gold in Guiana, and bad weather prevented the vessel from getting to an anchorage in Virginia.

Two further rescue attempts were made to Roanoke in 1599 and 1602, but on the first occasion the vessel was prevented from getting past the Outer Banks by bad weather, and on the second occasion no sign of the settlers could be found.

Then in March 1603 Queen Elizabeth died and at the very same time so did what remained of Raleigh's status. James I immediately dismissed him from his post as Captain of the Palace Guard. Within three months he was accused of plotting with one Lord Cobham to depose James I and replace him on the throne with Lady Arabella Stuart, who, it was intended, would make peace with Spain, which was of course a complete heresy, and permit Roman Catholic toleration in England, which was also heresy. Raleigh was tried before Chief Justice Popham of the Common Pleas. He was convicted of treason, after the jury had been out for half an hour, on the strength of one unsigned statement by Cobham who confessed his own guilt as to that conspiracy and implicated Raleigh. In spite of Raleigh's complaints as to the insufficiency of the evidence and his request to cross-examine Cobham, this was refused. The prosecution was conducted by the Attorney General, Sir Edward Coke, in a most intemperate manner. Raleigh was condemned to death in these words:

> You are to be conveyed to the place from whence you came and from thence to the place of execution, and there to be hanged till you are half dead, your members to be cut off, your bowels to be taken out and caste into the fire before your face (you being yet alive) your head to be cut off, your quarters to be divided into four parts, to be bestowed in four several places, and so (said my Lord Chief Justice) Lord have mercy upon your soul.

Shortly after I had been invited to come on this trip, I found a 1648 edition of some notes taken at Raleigh's trial which contained verbatim passages from what passed, including the one that I have just quoted. It is clear that it was a completely unfair trial and I think you will appreciate this from the other passages that I am going to read out from it.

Of the opening by Sir Edward Coke, this was said:

> In Mr Attorney diverse things were observed which were said and used in his narration or evidence. Some captiously noted that he said this treason did tend not only to overthrow of true religion and destruction of all our souls but even to the loss of our goods, lands and lives: but it seemeth he meant reciprocally: others thought him full of impertinent phrases and compliments, and especially when he spoke of the King's issue or of the Lords after he said he would say nothing of

> them, then he would presently fall into gross and palpable adulation of them to their faces but in their commendations he spoke nothing but truth.

A little further on, the note continues with regard to Coke's opening:

> All the assembly could have wished that he had not behaved himself so violently and bitterly nor used so great provocation to the prisoner which the better sort imputed to his zeal in the King's service and to the passion which overwhelmed him in the cause of his country as when he break forth into these and the like speeches: This horrible and detestable Traytor, this maine Traytor (for the rest were upon the bye), this instigator and seducer to treasons he that hath a Spanish heart, you are an odious man, see with what a whorish forehead he defends his faults. This is he that would take away the King and his cubs, oh abominable Traytor: but many prejudicate of Mr Attorney's nature would hardly be persuaded but those speeches proceeded out of the insolency of his own disposition given to triumph upon poor delinquents and men in misery. Honest men have reason to think the best and as the Attorney was noted so was the carriage of Raleigh most remarkable first to the Lords (principally to My Lord Cecil) humble yet not prostrate dutiful, yet not dejected for in some cases he would humbly thank them for gracious speeches, in other acknowledged that their honours said true as in relating some circumstances.

Then it was further said of Raleigh:

> But when it was insinuated that it was said that it would never be well until the King and his cubs were taken away he said that Mr Attorney used him basely, barbarously and rigorously and that he was a base slave and wretch that spoke the words, that he received comfort in these base words of Mr Attorney for he had hoped that it should be the worst that he should be able to do against him.

Later in the course of the trial the note records:

> And my Lord Chief Justice said that one witness accusing himself too was very great testimony especially in this case for it was not to be imagined that my Lord Cobham would do himself so much harm as to adventure the loss of his honour, lands of so great worth and his life for any spleen to Sir Walter unless the matter were true and therefore the accusation was very strong against Sir Walter.

Still later Raleigh has reported to have said this:

> But said he you tell me of one witness let me have him. Prove these practices by one witness and I will confess myself guilty to the King in a thousand treasons. I stand not upon the law, I defy the law if I have done these things I desire not to live: whether they be treasons by the law or no. Let me have my accuser brought to my face and if he will maintain it to my face I will confess my judgement.

Then the Lord Chief Justice, having been required to signify his opinion of the law on the evidence in this case, is reported to have said:

> It was not the law to have the witness brought to his face, considering he accused himself also: to the which the rest of the judges agreed. Sir Walter replied: it was not against or contrary to the law: howsoever I do not expect it of duty and yet

> I say you should deal very severely with me if you should condemn me and not bring my accuser to my face.

And then a little later in the note it says this:

> Why then my Lords let my accuser be brought and let me ask him a question and I have done: for it may be it will appear out of his own tale that his accusation cannot be true or he will be discovered by examination … If my accuser were dead, or not within the land, it was something. But my accuser lives, and is in the house, and yet you will not bring him to my face.

In his final speech to the jury Raleigh said this:

> If you would be content to be judged upon suspicions and inferences, if you would not have your accusation subscribed by your accuser. If you would not have your accuser brought to your face (being in the same house too) where you are arraigned. If you would be condemned by an accusation of one recanted and truly sorrowful for it, if you in my case would yield your bodies to torture, lose your lives, your wives and children and all your fortune upon so slender proof. Then I am ready to suffer all these things.

Although Raleigh had for many years become unpopular with the people because of his ostentation and conspicuous consumption, his conviction gave rise to enormous popular indignation, so great that James I was advised by Cecil to commute the death sentence. That left Raleigh in the Tower for 14 years, having been stripped of his Virginia monopoly and his lease of Durham House. During that time in December 1606 Captain Newport embarked upon yet another settlement expedition to Virginia. This one, astonishingly, was under the control of none other than Chief Justice Popham. The expedition arrived within the Outer Banks at the end of April 1607. A settlement in the name of James I was then declared at Jamestown. It is right to say that James I was totally disinterested in settlement in North America. Raleigh, however, had acted as unofficial consultant to the expedition, even from his quarters in the Tower. In his 'Essay on Colonisation' he wrote that settlers should educate the native people in law and religion and 'instruct them in the liberal arts of civility'.

Ten years later James I was so short of money that in 1617 he released Raleigh from the Tower in order for him to lead an expedition to the Orinoco River to try once again to take possession of the goldmine said to exist at Manoa. It was, however, a condition of that expedition that there was to be no invasion of Spanish territory, for James was then determined to negotiate a peace treaty with Spain. The expedition got to the Orinoco but Raleigh remained onboard and sent his second in command upstream with soldiers to find the goldmine. Completely contrary to orders, they carried out an attack on the Spanish garrison at San Thome. The attack was only partially successful and the expedition to be abandoned at that point. Raleigh then returned to London and was at once thrown into the Tower.

James I, to whom the Spanish ambassador had complained, immediately revoked the reprieve on Raleigh's death sentence. On 29 October Raleigh was executed at Westminster Old Palace.

Here is one final thought. According to an old diary of mine, on 21 June 1989 COMBAR was founded in principle at a meeting in the Devereux public house, which was built on what was originally the garden of Elizabeth's favourite, Robert Devereux, Earl of Essex, only a few hundred yards from the site of Raleigh's Durham House on the Embankment.

I can only say that it is good to see that our transatlantic aspirations have so excellently succeeded where Raleigh's proved so hard to achieve.

3

A New Life in the New World

SIR DAVID STEEL

Sir David Steel was also a guest judge of COMBAR in Virginia at the 2007 annual North American meeting, and gave this talk at lunchtime to the COMBAR delegates. Sir David Steel was the first Chairman of COMBAR, 1989–91. He is an arbitrator at Quadrant Chambers.

IT IS A great privilege for Charlotte and me to be your guests of honour at this unique meeting. It is also a pleasure to share that privilege with Tony and Angela Colman.

I think Tony and I can be justly proud of our child, borne over 15 years ago. The initial features of COMBAR which I believe have resulted in its continuing success and buoyancy are twofold. First, the decision that it should be properly financed, so as to ensure a professional secretariat. Second, the decision that membership should be primarily by sets of chambers rather than individuals, so as to ensure support across the whole spectrum of age and experience.

Any organisation with long-term aims must encourage the young, and I regard COMBAR's focus on this as having been conspicuously successful. Nonetheless, we now live in a world where a 21-year-old is almost treated as a child. How different things were 400 years ago.

Let us take John Smith, who had been on board one of the three vessels which set out from London in December 1606, bound for Virginia with 140 hopeful colonists. We will see his statue tomorrow, gazing out over the James River at the site of Jamestown.

Smith had been born in 1580. He left home at 16. He immediately volunteered to fight for the Dutch seeking their independence from Spain. Thereafter, having spent about two years at sea, in 1600 he joined the Austrian army in order to fight against the Turks. He became an army Captain at the age of 20.

Aged 22 he could be found fighting in Transylvania. However he was wounded, captured and sold as a slave to a Turk. The Turk sent him to Istanbul as a gift to his girlfriend. The girlfriend fell in love with him, but thereafter sent her brother to John Smith for army training. Captain Smith murdered the brother and escaped via Russia and Poland. He arrived back in England in 1604 at the ripe old age of 24. He was thus still in his twenties as the three vessels reached Virginia in 1606.

What remarkable courage was required to start a new life in the New World. The three ships had taken six weeks to get from England; 45 had died on the voyage, leaving 100 men and four boys. During the voyage Smith had managed to get arrested for mutiny and was sentenced to hang. However, on landing, Smith's name emerged from secret orders as one of the designated Councillors for the colony, thus leading to his reprieve.

What met the colonists ashore may have left those who had died en route feeling fortunate. Disease was rampant: typhus, malaria and dysentery; food was in desperately short supply, most of the water was unfit to drink, it was bitterly cold in winter and blisteringly hot in summer.

Needless to say, Smith was soon in trouble and managed to get himself captured by the Indians in October 1607. Facing almost inevitable death he somehow succeeded in obtaining his reprieve by showing his magnetic compass to the Indian chief Powatan.

It is ironic that the success of the colony was assured by two things which are regarded with such total disfavour today—tobacco and slavery. Again, it is the youth of the participants which is so striking.

John Rolfe had survived a shipwreck off Bermuda in 1609. He was 24. He had come on to Virginia in a vessel built from the wreckage of the other vessels (a story immortalised by William Shakespeare in *The Tempest*) but found only 60 survivors at Jamestown.

Although Jamestown was nearly abandoned, by 1612 Rolfe had begun growing tobacco. He had obtained the seeds of *nicotiana tabacum* from South America. By 1614 the prospects of the colony were dramatically transformed by the first shipment of tobacco to arrive in London. In the meantime Rolfe had married Pocahontas, the daughter of Powhatan bringing a prolonged period of peace with the Indians.

By 1635 Rolfe's son Thomas had reclaimed his father's tobacco plantations and the thousands of acres that were owned by his grandfather Powhatan. Tom Rolfe thus became the greatest landowner in Virginia. From the Rolfes are descended the great families of Virginia like the Randolphs, the Lewises, the Bollings and—wait for it—the Blairs.

By 1619 the cash crop of tobacco had led to a boom. So much so that 20 slaves were imported from Africa to help with the crops and 90 women from England to help with the population. The women were more expensive. They were 120lbs of tobacco each.

It is a fascinating tale. But I have said enough. I have very much in mind the advice of the mother whale to its offspring: 'Remember, it is while you are spouting that you are most likely to be harpooned.'

4

Bygone Days

STEVEN ROSENFELD

The North American meeting 2009 took place in Chicago. The dinner at the end of the meeting was held at the Art Institute in the reconstructed Stock Exchange Trading Room (the original Stock Exchange was demolished in 1972). Sections of elaborate decorations, moulded plaster capitals and art glass have been preserved from the Trading Room, and made a stunning back drop for the dinner.

The guest speaker at the North American dinner was Robert L Byman of Jenner & Block LLP. He was introduced by Steven Rosenfeld, a retired partner from the New York office of Paul, Weiss, Rifkind, Wharton & Garrison LLP. Steve practised in a variety of areas, with emphasis on securities, insurance and reinsurance, and complex trust and estate disputes. This being the 20th North American meeting, however, Steve also took the opportunity to reminisce, very entertainingly indeed, about the meetings which had taken place over the preceding years. By popular demand, therefore, we include below an edited version of Steve Rosenfeld's remarks. Emphasis is added by the author.

Hi, everyone. I'm Steve Rosenfeld, and I'm the 'warm-up act'.

Before I begin, I want to compliment Stephen Moriarty on the superb job he's done as Chair of the North American Committee, both last year in Berlin and here in Chicago. He's brought these annual meetings to a new level of excellence that will be a standard to meet as we go forward.

Needless to say, I was very pleased when Stephen asked me to say a few words this evening. But I have been puzzled about exactly why it was that I was the one chosen to fill this particular slot on the programme for this 20th annual gathering. Did Stephen expect something new, provocative and exciting? That's surely not me—I've been around about as long as anyone.

As I thought about it, I concluded that what Stephen was looking for was the antithesis of something new. What he wanted after two days of hand-wringing about the global financial crisis was stability, consistency—someone who could take you back to the bygone days of the very first North American Committee meeting more than 19 years ago.

But Stephen overlooked one fact: when you get to be my age three things happen. The first is your memory goes … I can't remember the other two. Fortunately, though, here, as in so much that COMBAR does, the intrepid

Veronica Kendall came to my rescue—or I should say to Moriarty's. Veronica was able to email to me last week *all* of the programmes for these meetings except the first three. So, if you'll join me for a few minutes on a whirlwind tour through the past 20 years, you may find what you might view as some consistency in the range of subjects explored at these conferences, as well as some stability in the talent tapped as programme speakers.

Without the programmes, I can't tell you much about the first three meetings—except that they took place in London, Washington, and then back in London; my diaries say I attended all three; and I have a vague notion that among the topics was something about International Arbitration.

So let's skip to 1993—the Castle Harbour Hotel in Bermuda (unlike COMBAR, since totally demolished!). On the programme were panels on forum-shopping, banking regulation and ADR (including, of course, Arbitration). Among the speakers were chaps named Collins, McDougall, Jarvis, Blair, Powell and Barist. And the MOOT made its debut. Indeed, having suggested it, my reward was to argue in the first one. Back then, we didn't have *teams* in the moot: we had to go it alone, one on one—two Yanks arguing before a US judge, followed by the same case argued before the Rt Hon Lord Justice Andrew Leggatt, by two Brits named Bernard Rix QC and (yes, believe it or not) Peter Gross QC. Mr Justice Gross told me yesterday that he has absolutely no recollection whatever of that argument, so I'm safe in assuring you that it had something to do with a Chinese letter of credit—and that (perhaps in contrast to this morning's proceedings), we took the moot *damned seriously* in those days.

In 1994, we were in Paris. It rained, and rained, and rained. On top of which, the Metro was closed down by a strike so there were no cabs, and we were more or less stranded in the hotel. Can you picture it? There was Jeff Barist in Paris, and only hotel food to eat! There were panels on 'International Insolvency'—and again, a panel on Arbitration. The speakers included Steel, Collins, Higham and Knowles. And, again, a one-on-one moot, in which Barist, weakened by the quality of the cuisine, had to get up and argue a transfer of venue motion. I won't tell you if he won, or who the judge was—you'll have to ask Jeff.

1995 brought us to New York, to celebrate the 100th anniversary of the founding of the Commercial Court. There were also panels on insolvency, banking and, oh yes, Arbitration. And the roster of speakers included Messrs Jarvis, Knowles, Blair, McDougall, Barist, Collins and two new names from the US side: Eric Lewis and Mark Alcott. And instead of the moot, we visited a real jury trial in the Southern District of New York.

I missed the next meeting in London, but the programme says the theme was commercial fraud, on which there was expert input from none other than Jarvis, Knowles, Michael Brindle, Barbara Dohmann, Barist, Lewis, Alcott and, in his COMBAR debut, one F Paul Morrison (watch out for THAT name as we move along). And the contrasting US and UK moot returned—but this time, it was two against two.

Then on to Toronto, where we heard from Barist, Collins, Alcott, McDougall, Jarvis, Knowles, Higham, F Paul Morrison and newcomers Andrew Miller and Bryan Finlay, on such stimulating topics as 'UK Domestic Law Within the European Union: Canadian and US Federal/Provincial/State Comparisons' (wouldn't you know I got assigned to that panel?) and another panel on 'New Developments in (you guessed it) Arbitration Law'.

In 1998, the Committee FINALLY figured out what brought people to these curious conclaves, and we found ourselves in ... VENICE! Ah Venice—now THAT was a meeting to remember: the food, the art, the palazzos, even the speakers, including Blair, Jarvis, Powell, Higham, Collins, Barist, McDougall, Miller, Alcott, F Paul Morrison and the first appearance of a youngster named Earl Cherniak.

The next year the meeting made a return visit to Washington where—on the heels of the Clinton impeachment trial, the Committee chose the theme of ... ETHICS! About which much wisdom was elicited from the likes of Barist, Miller, Lewis, Finlay, Cherniak, Knowles, Dohmann—and F Paul Morrison. The moot was like this morning's a demonstration of comparative styles of cross-examination, but there was a difference: picking up on the Clinton/Lewinsky affair, the task was to cross-examine a young intern about whether or not she did it with her boss and, if so, where, how, and who started it. I couldn't attend, but I am reliably informed that Jarvis QC—who drew the assignment from the UK side—just couldn't bring himself to ask any really probing questions. JL McDougall, on the other hand, had no trouble getting right to the point!

Back to London in 2000, featuring an elegant black tie dinner at the Locarno Suite of the Foreign & Commonwealth Office; panels on international jurisdiction, e-commerce and human rights, to which the contributors included Dohmann, McDougall, Barist, Cherniak, Lewis and F Paul Morrison—and there was a moot about fraud (with the teams now expanded to three against three).

In 2001, we hit the beach in Grand Cayman, but still found time between tennis and sunbathing to listen to Dohmann, Brindle, Ali Malek, Blair, Barist, Lewis, Jarvis, McDougall, Collins, Miller—and F Paul Morrison—hold forth on topics like fraud, International Insolvency and Alternative Dispute Resolution (aka arbitration) and we saw the first appearance, as the junior advocate in the moot, of none other than David Wingfield.

2002: Prague. Panels on commercial fraud, privilege, and expert evidence—featuring Blair, Hancock, Lewis, Cherniak, Alcott, McDougall, Jarvis and F Paul Morrison. A moot starring Barist, Malek, Finlay and David Wingfield. A rollicking after dinner speech by Andrew Miller, and a trip to the Prague State Opera to hear *Carmen* sung in Czech, with an American Escamillo who seemed to think the opera was *Frankenstein*.

Next, Boston. Among the topics: legal ethics, terrorist financing—and 'Interpretation of Arbitration Clauses'. Yes, there were appearances from

Brindle, Blair, Powell, McDougall, Collins, Alcott, Cherniak, Barist, Malek, Lewis, Jarvis, Wingfield—and F Paul Morrison. And who can forget that sublime cocktail cruise in Boston Harbour? Not John Jarvis, who took one sip of the jug wine being offered, and threatened to jump overboard and swim back to the hotel.

Barcelona in 2004 brought us panels on concurrent proceedings, privilege, ethical issues and insolvency, with input from, inter alia, Miller, Alcott, Knowles, Hancock, Jarvis, Cherniak, McDougall, an after-dinner speech by Jeffrey Barist at that gorgeous private estate, Bel Reco (discovered by Ali Malek), and the next day, a moot featuring the fierce advocacy of, inter alia, Dohmann, Finlay, Wingfield—and F Paul Morrison. The topic? International … Arbitration!

Then it was San Francisco. The panellists included Hancock, Cherniak, Wingfield, Jarvis, Lewis, and Barist. The 'moot' (if you can call it that) was a stunner: a mock *case management conference*—I kid you not—before (get this) *three* judges (one of whom was Michael Collins)—a difficult assignment that naturally demanded contending teams of advocates increased to FIVE per side—including of course, F Paul Morrison.

I missed Rome in 2006, but Veronica's programme says you heard from Wingfield, Barist, Brindle, McDougall, Collins, Finlay, Dohmann—and F Paul Morrison. There was a private visit to the newly refurbished Sistine Chapel, but the highlight must surely have been that panel on 'Cultural Differences in Arbitration'.

The 400th anniversary of the founding of the Jamestown colony brought us to Richmond, Virginia in 2007 to celebrate, not the cannibalism allegedly practised by the Jamestown colonists, but the transport of the common law to the New World. There were speeches by people with 'Honourable Justice' legitimately in front of their names—like Steel, Colman, O'Connor and of course, panel presentations by (among others) Blair, Miller, Malek, Alcott, McDougall, Wingfield and Lewis (yes, yes, including one on 'Transnational Investment Arbitration').

Which brings me to last year in Berlin, where the weather was hot, the subject was 'Combating Fraud and Corruption', a topic on which where was no shortage of knowledge, including by Dohmann, Brindle, Finlay, Barist, Wingfield, Cherniak—and F Paul Morrison. We had dinner atop the Reichstag and a cocktail cruise on the Spree River, and this time Jarvis drank the wine and remained on board.

I don't know if John would have plunged into the Chicago River last evening, but I do know that he missed this year's terrific presentations on the financial crisis by, among others, Wingfield, Finlay, Powell, Collins, Cherniak—and at least a paper authored by F Paul Morrison who, had he not been detained in Toronto on a trial, would have made his record-setting *14th* appearance at a North American Committee meeting. Congratulations Paul!

So that ends the whirlwind tour. But those of you who, like me, found it a pleasant nostalgia trip know that it hasn't been us repeat offenders who have made these annual meetings consistently stimulating, challenging and, yes, entertaining. Rather, it's been all the younger members of COMBAR on both sides of the ocean, who in increasing numbers contribute new ideas and fresh approaches. They are really what keeps the old guys like me coming back year after year ... and so I salute them.

And speaking of fresh faces, we now come to the REAL reason I'm even up here: to introduce our proper after-dinner speaker, Robert Byman. And I'm pleased and happy to do that.

Bob is a litigation partner of the leading Chicago law firm of Jenner & Block. I'll just give you a smattering of the *extensive* information you can find out about him on his firm's website (that's www.jenner.com, if you want to look). He earned both his BA and JD degrees at the University of Illinois, where he was Student Body President *and* an editor of the Illinois Law Forum. He's a Regent of the American College of Trial Lawyers and has (it says at www.jenner.com) 'tried dozens of cases to jury or bench verdict in a gamut of substantive areas, including patents and intellectual property, commodities and securities, trade practices, environmental, employment, land use, professional liability, civil rights, and a wide variety of complex contractual disputes'. WOW!

I'm a bit reluctant to tell you this next part, but, having heard yesterday's panels, I suppose I'd better make full disclosure of our risks. The Jenner & Block website says that: 'Mr Byman has extensive experience ... as an arbitrator ... has been a member of the Commercial Arbitration Panel of the American Arbitration Association since 1978 and has served as an arbitrator in dozens of AAA cases.'

Bob also writes a column every now and again for the *National Law Journal*—together with his partner Jerry Solovy. I've read a few of them, and while they all get across serious points about lawyers and lawyering, the tone is always breezy, irreverent, and usually very funny. I don't know if that entertaining style comes from Solovy or Byman, but we're about to find out.

So here to talk to us about arbitration—no, just kidding, about some aspects of the financial crisis, is Robert L Byman.

5

The Abuse of Power

SIR STEPHEN SEDLEY

In October 2011 Sir Stephen Sedley delivered the Annual COMBAR Lecture at Middle Temple Hall.

ONCE UPON A time, in a small town in the Midlands which has now vanished into the Birmingham conurbation, a Sabbatarian group secured a majority on the local council. One of their aims was to halt the growing disregard of Sunday as a day of rest and prayer and the use of the Sabbath for secular entertainment. So, when the company which owned the local Gaumont cinema applied to the council for permission to open on Sundays, they granted the application, since they had no good reason not to, but made it a condition that the permission was not to include children under 15. For the Sabbatarians this was a very satisfactory condition because it meant that, unless they were prepared to leave their children unsupervised in the house (this was before the days of universal domestic television), parents would not be able to go to the cinema on Sundays either. Effectively the councillors had succeeded in keeping the local cinema closed on the Sabbath.

The Sunday observance laws had since the late eighyteenth century forbidden Sunday entertainments. But by the 1940s the cinema had become a mass entertainment medium. To enable them to open on a Sunday, the one day when most working people were able to go, Parliament in 1932 passed the Sunday Entertainments Act, allowing local authorities to lift the ban on Sunday entertainments on such conditions as each authority thought fit to impose. This was the power which the Wednesbury councillors—for it was they—used when in 1947 they purported to allow the cinema in Walsall Street to open on Sundays.

It was not surprising that Associated Provincial Picture Houses, who a few years earlier had spent a small fortune upgrading the Walsall Street cinema to a state-of-the-art Gaumont picture palace, took exception to this and went off to the High Court to challenge it. The argument was straightforward enough: if, as was uncontested, it was appropriate to let the Gaumont open on Sundays, it was a misuse of the statutory power to annex a condition which had nothing to do with either physical or moral safety and much to do with religious doctrine, and which meant that the permission granted with one hand was being taken away with the other.

Every law student knows what the Court of Appeal said about the law; but one wonders how many of them know what the court actually decided?[1] Associated Provincial Picture Houses lost in the High Court, and lost again in the Court of Appeal. Not for the first or last time, the court set out a shining set of principles on which it would unhesitatingly restrain abuses of power, and then declined to apply any of them to the facts before it.

In its time and place, this was unsurprising. For reasons which are still not fully explored or understood, judicial review of governmental action, which had been developed and refined by the Victorian judges, fell into a long sleep after 1914, from which it has awoken only in our lifetime. In the course of it, a succession of challenges to the way in which the power created by the 1932 Act was being deployed or manipulated by local authorities had come before the courts, but effectively all of them had failed. So disused had public law become that the *Wednesbury* case itself was brought not by application for a prerogative writ, but by an ordinary civil action for a declaration that the resolution was ultra vires and unreasonable. The judicial response, well exemplified by the decision, was that government, both central and local, was to be left to get on with its job without an over-nice regard to the legality of what it was doing. In a period in which stable governments were rare and the country was having to be run by senior civil servants who outranked most ministers in experience and competence, such a judicial policy was intelligible. But it meant, when in 1947 Lord Greene came to deliver his judgment on the Wednesbury affair after a weekend's reflection, that the principles he was able to recite from his own training in public law in the halcyon days before the Great War were not going to be enough to bring about any interference with the council's eccentric resolution.

Like its protagonists, the *Wednesbury* decision itself has merged into history. The borough in 1974 became part of the borough of Sandwell, and the Gaumont in Walsall Street became a bingo hall. I do not believe that any modern court of judicial review would allow a public authority's decision like the Wednesbury resolution to stand. It might be held to be vitiated by the council's attempt to enforce a view of how young persons should spend their Sundays which lay beyond its remit—in other words, by an irrelevant consideration. But it would almost certainly be struck down because of the annexure of a condition which made the permission itself practically worthless. If, in other words, the councillors had had a good reason for not permitting the Gaumont to open on Sundays, they could and should have simply refused to allow it; but, evidently having no such reason, they could not logically allow Sunday opening and in the next breath stifle it. The resolution, to use Lord Greene's taxonomy, was irrational.

[1] *Associated Provincial Picture Houses v Wednesbury Corporation* [1948] 1 KB 223.

There is today much less emphasis on Lord Greene's pigeonholes, and rightly so. First of all, they are far from being a complete account of how public law stood even in the doldrum years. They omit, for example, the use of a power for a collateral or improper purpose, a vice which the Victorian judges had clearly identified. Today it is generally accepted that the defining question in modern public law is whether the impugned official action represents an abuse of power.

We have got here by a long and circuitous route. The power of the High Court to strike down or prohibit unauthorised acts of government and to require the repair of unlawful omissions was well established by the sixteenth century. But it was not until the mid-nineteenth century that the growing need for statutory regulation of Britain's booming industrial and commercial society gave powers to boards, commissions and inspectorates whose notions of due process and whose understanding of their own remits were not the same as the courts'.

Lawyers and judges took the short cut of describing the courts' supervisory role in the Latin phrase *ultra vires*, a concept which was already bringing company law into disrepute by allowing limited liability companies to renege on their contractual obligations by pleading their own incapacity to enter into them. But the metaphor of a governmental body, whether national or local, elected or appointed, as a company with prescribed powers was never a very satisfactory one. If taken literally, as it too often was, it led the courts to ignore transgressions which could not be matched against a real or supposed rulebook. Frequently the relevant rules were not prescribed by the donor of the power, but derived from what Mr Justice Byles famously described, in 1863, as the justice of the common law. When a builder named Cooper put up a house in Wandsworth without notifying the local Board of Works, and the Board razed it to the ground without first hearing what he had to say about it, the fact that the empowering statute had omitted to provide for anything resembling a hearing was held not to matter: what mattered was that to act in such a way was an abuse of power, and the courts were there to stop it.[2]

Nobody doubts that power—any power—can be abused; and nobody is likely to assert that abusing it is a good thing. Like sin, we are all against it. We all know, too, that Lord Acton wrote: 'PPower tends to corrupt, and absolute power corrupts absolutely',[3] though why a casual line in a letter to a bishop should have achieved such celebrity is something of a mystery. Even more mysterious is what was going on in the mind of the Dragon Lady, the late Madame Nhu, when she remarked half a century ago: 'Power is delightful, and absolute power is absolutely delightful'. But whether she was

[2] *Cooper v Wandsworth Board of Works* (1863) 14 CB (NS) 180.

[3] *The life and letters of Mandell Creighton* (1904), reproducing a letter of 3 April 1887 from Acton.

neatly parodying Lord Acton or innocently misquoting him, she knew what she was talking about. As the sister-in-law of the South Vietnamese dictator Ngo Dinh Diem, Mme Nhu had accumulated powers which, according to one American commentator, were the equivalent of simultaneously running the CIA, the FBI, the Congress and the press.

An autocrat can do almost anything without exceeding his powers. In a state which acknowledges the rule of law, by contrast, there are multiple constraints on the exercise of power. Breaking these bounds may attract political or public censure but is not necessarily a justiciable abuse. Nor, however, is the abuse of power necessarily deliberate or reckless. It may happen by pure inadvertence, as it probably did in Wandsworth; it may be done, as it most often is, for political advantage; very rarely its motive may be corrupt; or—as Mme Nhu reminded the world—it may be done, as arguably it was in Wednesbury, for the sheer satisfaction of doing it.

I want to consider such abuses, though without assigning any single motive to them, in three contemporary contexts, none of them the now familiar context of judicial review. One is the possible misuse of Parliament's own constitutional supremacy. The second is the misuse by ministers of the royal prerogative. The third, arguably the most insidious, is the use of the power of communication, both in governmental and in private hands, in order to disinform.

I have first to excuse my failure to include the judiciary in this sweep of the searchlight. Thanks to a visceral and no doubt misplaced sense of loyalty to a bench on which I sat for nearly two decades, I am in a poor position to take an objective look at it. But I am certainly conscious of its vulnerability to abuse. Sitting in Room 101 (presciently nominated by George Orwell as the place where the thing you most dread happens to you), I used regularly to be asked to grant injunctions to freeze the assets of claimants' business competitors who were alleged to owe them money—a form of order which, as claimants well knew, could put a small business swiftly on the rocks. The application, made in the nature of things in the defendant's absence, was commonly supported by an affidavit, sworn by or derived from an enquiry agent, containing complete details of the defendant's bank accounts. I began to make a practice of asking counsel for an assurance, on instructions, that this information had been lawfully obtained. If it had not been, I would refuse to make an order, because the claimant had not come to court with clean hands. I never once received an affirmative answer to my question. The *News of the World* débacle has now confirmed why, but the use not only by journalists but by lawyers of private investigators with ready access to corrupt officials and police officers is not new. The legal profession bears blame for turning a profitably blind eye to it; but I think too that the judges could and should have done more to root it out.

Nor am I going to be saying much about the use by ministers of their status to attack judges whose decisions they dislike. When a prime minister,

Tony Blair, feels free to attack a judge, Mr Justice Sullivan, for having 'taken leave of his senses' in a decision on the Afghan plane hijackers which was unanimously upheld by the Court of Appeal; and when a Home Secretary, Teresa May, with her own prime minister's backing, attacks the Supreme Court in very similar language over a cautious and balanced decision that not all sex offenders need remain on the register for life, something is going wrong with the rule of law and the separation of powers: far from judges seeking to influence the political process, politicians appear to be seeking to influence the judicial process.

All that I propose to say about this culture of ministerial abuse is that its seriousness was recognised by the Select Committee on the Constitution in its 2007 report, which advised that the next revision of the Ministerial Code, which Downing Street periodically issues, should contain strongly worded guidelines about public comment by ministers on individual judges. Yet the Code today still contains nothing about ministerial attacks on judicial decisions. One can speculate about the reasons for this omission, but they are unlikely to be divorced from the fact that ministerial attacks on judges play well with much of the press.

Parliament's supremacy in our constitution is not today in question, though more than one academic commentator and more than one judge has suggested that its legislative power is not unlimited. But supreme power, whether or not subject to formal limits, carries a high degree of responsibility. One such responsibility is not to misuse the immunities which the parliamentary function necessarily attracts. Another is to maintain the separation of the state's powers, of which parliamentary sovereignty is one element only: another element, judicial independence, is no less important.

The latter of these obligations might at one time have been dismissed as mere aspiration, but since the enactment of section 3 of the 2005 Constitutional Reform Act, ministers have been under an explicit statutory duty to uphold the independence of the judiciary. It may yet become necessary to test whether the duty is enforceable. All one can do for the present is note that in 2007 the House of Lords Select Committee on the Constitution, reporting on the wave of ministerial attacks on judges, spoke of:

> the need for an independent judiciary able to interpret the laws made by Parliament, particularly when Ministers do not appear to understand the constraints that apply to their policies, or indeed the full content of legislation that they proposed to parliament.[4]

Article 9 of the 1689 Bill of Rights, one of the foundational documents of our democracy, forbids the impeachment or questioning in any court or place out of Parliament of 'the freedom of speech and debates or proceedings in Parlyament'. The protection that this gave to a courageous member

[4] HL Paper 151, 26 July 2007, para 55.

like Samuel Plimsoll in his campaign for safe merchant shipping, conducted in a Parliament stuffed with shipping interests, has been amply justified. But the necessary quid pro quo was, at least until recently, a reciprocal recognition by both Houses of Parliament that they were not to defy or impugn the decisions of the courts—something constitutionally distinct from the practice of ministerial briefings against individual judges. The reason was and is that it is the courts and not Parliament who have the sovereign function of interpreting and applying the law. If members object to the courts' decisions, their recourse is to persuade Parliament to change the law, possibly even retrospectively. If they consider a judge of the senior courts unfit for office, he or she may be removed on an address of both Houses of Parliament, but not otherwise.[5]

Some of this historic settlement has threatened to fall apart with the deliberate naming in the Upper and Lower Houses earlier this year of two claimants whose identity had been expressly protected by court orders. It is unsurprising that the media, from whom such disclosures earn applause, at worst cheered and at best equivocated. But it is both surprising and disturbing that the Speakers of both Houses, especially the Commons, where the Speaker has disciplinary powers, appear to have done nothing to call the two members to account for the use of parliamentary privilege to avoid prosecution for what appeared to have been a calculated contempt of court.

In 1996 a junior minister and member of the Bar, Neil Hamilton, issued proceedings for libel against the *Guardian* newspaper. He also sued Mohammed Al Fayed, who claimed to have paid him substantial sums of money for asking parliamentary questions. (Evidently nobody had told Mr Al Fayed that if you have a sensible question for a minister, your MP will ask it free of charge.) On a preliminary application, a Queen's Bench judge ruled that the case against the *Guardian*, as pleaded, could not be tried without infringing article 9 of the Bill of Rights. There was no interlocutory appeal against the decision. Instead, an amendment was moved to the Defamation Bill then before Parliament, permitting an MP or peer (or for that matter a witness before a parliamentary committee) who was involved in defamation proceedings to waive, 'so far as concerns him, the protection of any enactment ... which prevents proceedings in Parliament being impeached or questioned in any court'—in other words, to disapply article 9 of the Bill of Rights in his or her own personal interests.

Although the Lord Chancellor had moved other amendments to the Bill, he did not move this one. On Lord Mackay's invitation it was moved by Lord Hoffmann, and in spite of principled opposition in the Upper House from distinguished lawyers and historians, who pointed out that article 9 was there to protect the legislature as a body, not to give individual members

[5] Originally laid down in the Act of Settlement 1700.

a weapon which they could use as it suited them, it was passed in both Houses.

Neil Hamilton, having used the waiver to continue with his action against the Guardian, abandoned the case shortly before trial. He went on to lose his libel action against Mohammed Al Fayed, in circumstances which were both dramatic and ironic. Mr Al Fayed failed in his attempt to get the action stayed on the ground that it could not be properly tried without infringing the Bill of Rights: this, the House of Lords held, was taken care of by Mr Hamilton's own waiver. Then, shortly before the jury trial, it came to the knowledge of Mr Al Fayed's lawyers that Mr Hamilton had a few years earlier tabled an amendment to a Finance Bill which, although later withdrawn, would have improved the tax position of oil companies, including Mobil, whom he had been advising as junior counsel. He had subsequently billed Mobil for a fee of £10,000. A late amendment of the defence was allowed in order to plead the receipt of this money as a corrupt act, and the jury in due course returned an affirmative answer to the judge's question: 'Are you satisfied ... that Mr Hamilton was corrupt in his capacity as a Member of Parliament?' Whether the answer was based on Mr Al Fayed's allegation that Mr Hamilton had been collecting cash in brown envelopes in return for placing questions, or on the Mobil episode (which depended not at all on Mr Al Fayed's testimony), or on both, we cannot know for sure, though the Court of Appeal later took the view that Mr Hamilton's chance of weathering the Mobil evidence was slender.[6] But the irony is that, had it not been for Mr Hamilton's earlier decision to waive the protection of the Bill of Rights in his own interests, it might not have been possible for his tabling of a parliamentary amendment to be called in question by Mr Al Fayed, by way of defence to his libel proceedings.

Not long after the libel action, in 1999, the Joint Committee on Parliamentary Privilege advised that the provision which had been slotted into the Defamation Act should be repealed and any power of waiver be placed in the hands of each House; but, in spite of opportunities to reverse it, in 2011 it is still on the statute book. If the reason is that, notwithstanding its distorting effect on the constitution, parliamentarians are content to leave it there for a rainy day, they might reflect that those who live by such a waiver can also perish by it.

One of the most important discrete powers of the state is adjudication. For self-evident reasons this function, in any society which respects the rule of law, has to be in the hands of competent judges who decide cases free of pressure from either executive government or the legislature. Until not long ago it was possible to point to this as a uniformly respected principle of our constitution.

[6] *Hamilton v Al Fayed* [2001] EMLR 394 (CA).

Then in 2004, the government promoted an Asylum and Immigration Bill which contained two highly controversial clauses. One was a radical privative clause which would have shut off all appeal to the regular courts and all judicial review of asylum and immigration decisions. It provoked a predictable storm of academic and professional outrage. Ronald Dworkin, in a lecture delivered in Cambridge, urged the judiciary to refuse to implement it if it was passed; Lord Woolf spoke out publicly against it; and in the end it was dropped. But it had succeeded in what a hardened cynic, unlike me, might have suspected was its real purpose: to distract attention from a second highly objectionable clause, clause 8, which was duly and quietly passed into law.

Although its principal target is the first-instance judges in the asylum appeal system, the provision binds the appellate courts which have to consider the tenability of their determinations. Section 8, as it now is, of the 2004 Act concerns claimants' credibility.

> (1) In determining whether to believe a statement made by or on behalf of a person who makes an asylum claim or a human rights claim, a deciding authority shall take account, as damaging the claimant's credibility, of any behaviour to which this section applies.
> (2) This section applies to any behaviour by the claimant that the deciding authority thinks—
> (a) is designed or likely to conceal information,
> (b) is designed or likely to mislead, or
> (c) designed or likely to obstruct or delay the handling or resolution of the claim or the taking of a decision in relation to the claimant.

The enactment so far appears to be addressed to immigration judges who were born yesterday. Although on its face it applies to Home Office and Border Agency officials too, there was no conceivable need for them to be directed by primary legislation. This was the delivery of a demeaning lecture to a tranche of the judiciary. On it went:

> (3) Without prejudice to the generality of subsection (2) the following kinds of behaviour shall be treated as designed or likely to conceal information or to mislead—
> (a) failure without reasonable explanation to produce a passport on request to an immigration officer or to the Secretary of State,
> (b) the production of a document which is not a valid passport as if it were,

and so on, through a series of acts and omissions—destroying documents, refusing to answer questions, failing to seek asylum in other safe countries or to apply for it on arrival here—which could have been captioned 'Instructions to grandmothers on how to suck eggs'. But slotted into it was the mandate I have quoted, to disbelieve the evidence of someone who has used a false passport to enter this country in order to seek asylum. Unlike the other forms of suspect behaviour, this one carries no 'reasonable explanation' proviso. In some cases there may in truth be no good excuse for using false papers; but in others, among them the most serious, there may have been no other way of escaping a despotic regime. Yet the legislation sought to interfere with the already difficult judicial function of deciding whether such a person's account of torture or persecution is true, by compelling judges, possibly contrary to their judicial oath, to hold against such people the very means by which they may have been forced to flee. It also had the unjust object of turning a foolish or manipulative act, such as making for the UK in preference to another safe country, into a ground for disbelieving what might be a perfectly truthful account of why the individual fled in the first place.

So far as I know, this attempt to use the legislative power not to set down the law the judges are to follow or to adjust the rules of evidence or procedure, but to direct judges how to find facts, a function which is constitutionally theirs alone, is unique. At least I hope so. But it was not a momentary aberration. The provision was the fulfilment of a public threat the Home Secretary, David Blunkett, had made in the spring of the previous year when, to a fanfare of abuse led by the *Daily Mail*, Mr Justice Collins had ruled that the Home Secretary was misapplying his own legislation in denying all benefits to asylum-seekers who in his view had failed to seek asylum on arrival, regardless of his own statutory obligation not to let individuals fall into a state of destitution amounting to cruel or inhuman treatment—an obligation specifically introduced into the legislation by the Home Secretary himself in order to respect the UK's international human rights obligations.

Mr Blunkett, seemingly forgetting this, told a radio interviewer that he was fed up with Parliament debating issues and judges overturning them. He also told the *Daily Telegraph* that judicial intervention was threatening democracy. He announced an immediate appeal. When it failed, his leading counsel told the Court of Appeal that there would be no further appeal and that the Home Secretary would be acting on the law as explained by the court. But departmental press briefings following the first-instance decision had by then made it clear that the government had already decided to introduce legislation to tie the hands of the judges. Hence the clause of the 2004 Bill that became section 8; and hence too, or so the cynic would speculate, the lightning conductor of the abandoned privative clause.

The rule of law, however, has proved robust enough to weather this squall. When the meaning of section 8 finally came before the Court of Appeal, counsel for the Home Secretary did not attempt to support its plain meaning. Both sides adopted the emollient ministerial explanation given to the Lords that 'The clause will not force a deciding authority to give undue weight to any of the factors it lists.' With this encouragement, the Court decided that the words requiring judges to treat the listed acts as damaging the claimant's credibility were to be read as if they said 'potentially damaging the claimant's credibility'. They did so on the ground that it was to be assumed that Parliament did not intend to interfere with judicial independence.[7] So it goes.

There is a second form of legislation, the Order in Council, which receives no parliamentary attention at all. Some Orders in Council are made under express statutory powers and rank as statutory instruments. Those providing for governance of the colonies, however, continue to be made by the Queen in Council as an exercise of the royal prerogative. They form a major exception to the rule, laid down four centuries ago in the *Case of Proclamations*,[8] that the Crown cannot legislate without the advice and consent of Parliament. They thus represent a form of ministerial power which Mme Nhu would have recognised as absolutely delightful, for the Privy Council does not even meet to discuss them, and the Monarch's assent to them is a constitutional formality.

In an article published in 1994, when he was still in opposition, Jack Straw wrote:

> The royal prerogative has no place in a modern western democracy ... [It] has been used as a smoke-screen by Ministers to obfuscate the use of power for which they are insufficiently accountable.[9]

It has nevertheless been one of the achievements of modern public law to bring the ministerial use of the royal prerogative within the reach of judicial review, starting in 1967 when the High Court asserted its supervisory jurisdiction over the first criminal injuries compensation scheme, which had been deliberately set up by the Home Office without enabling legislation, and culminating, ironically, in the confirmation by the House of Lords in the Chagos Islanders' case in 2008 that judicial review ran to the prerogative power to legislate by Order in Council for the colonies.

I say 'ironically' because the Chagos Islanders' case, like the *Wednesbury* case, failed to deliver on its legal promise. Having confirmed the view of the Divisional Court and the Court of Appeal[10] that prerogative Orders in Council are open to judicial review for abuse of power, a bare majority of the House declined to exercise the jurisdiction on facts which had seemed to seven other judges (potently among them Lord Bingham) to establish a clear and shameful abuse of power by the British government.[11] In 2000 a Divisional Court had struck down as ultra vires a local ordinance purporting to exile the Chagossians from their islands, and the Foreign Secretary, Robin Cook, had undertaken to Parliament that the wrong would now be put right. For the time being, it was: the Chagossians were given a legal right

[7] *JT (Cameroon) v Home Secretary* [2008] EWCA Civ 878.
[8] *The Case of Proclamations* (1611) 1 Co Rep 74; 24 ER 646.
[9] In A Barnett (ed), *Power and the Throne: the monarchy debate* (1994).
[10] *Bancoult v Foreign Secretary* [2007] EWCA Civ 498; [2008] QB 365.
[11] [2008] UKHL 61; [2009] 1 AC 453.

of return. We still do not know what it was that four years later prompted some FCO officials to advise the Foreign Secretary to renege on his predecessor's honourable act and to do by Order in Council what the court had held could not be lawfully done by ordinance: exclude the Chagos Islanders for ever from their homeland. But we do know that the Foreign Secretary who did it was Jack Straw.[12]

The Chagos Islanders' case has a further bearing on my subject. In the *CCSU* case in 1984,[13] Lord Roskill listed a number of prerogative functions which in his view could never come within the purview of the courts: the making of treaties, the defence of the realm, the prerogative of mercy, the grant of honours, the dissolution of Parliament, the appointment of ministers. Giving judgment in the Court of Appeal in the Chagos Islanders' case, I ventured to wonder whether in the light of modern experience these examples all held good. Would the courts be powerless if it was proved to them that an honour was being granted in return for payment? Or if some future government proposed to embark on what was, under the Nuremberg principles, a war of aggression? Or if a Home Secretary used the royal pardon, or an Attorney-General the power to abandon a prosecution, for an illegal or improper reason? Or if a future prime minister sought to appoint a convicted fraudster to ministerial office, or refused to invite the Monarch to prorogue a Parliament which had run its course? If such things were ever to occur, people might think the law was deficient if the courts could not do anything about them.

Let me turn lastly to an area where it is very difficult indeed to envisage the courts being able to intervene—the power to disseminate information which is not true. The media and government share with private individuals the inestimable, albeit qualified, privilege of free speech. But while the individual today may have access through the web to what was once inaccessible dissemination, it is government and the media which still possess the megaphones. Free speech, as I said in the case of the evangelical street preachers, is a right which includes 'not only the inoffensive but the irritating, the contentious, the eccentric, the heretical, the unwelcome and the provocative, provided it does not tend to provoke violence'.[14] It also, more troublingly, includes the slapdash, the inaccurate and the downright mendacious, provided the untruth does not defame an individual or strike at the administration of justice.

Let me mention here one small instance of the distorting effect which the pressure on journalists to titillate rather than to educate has on the reporting of court decisions, and of how casual the gathering and reporting of news

12 See D Snoxell, (2008) 36 *Journal of Imperial and Commonwealth History*; (2009) 37 *Journal of Imperial and Commonwealth History*.

13 [1985] AC 374.

14 *Redmond-Bate v DPP* [2000] HRLR 249; (1999) 7 BHRC 375.

can become even in respectable quarters. When in 2003 Mr Justice Collins gave the controversial asylum law judgment which I have mentioned, I was telephoned by a BBC radio producer to ask if I would take part in a live discussion about the press furore. I said that I wouldn't, because judgments have to speak for themselves, and I assumed the producer had read this one. There was a pause. No, said the producer, he hadn't. Well has the presenter read it? Another pause. 'We're busy people, you know; I'm sure he'll try.' Did they have a copy of it, then? 'Well, no, but I'm sure we can get one.' At this point I took the conversation off the record, with the result that I am not at liberty to tell you what followed.

Instances of press stories which owe more to a combination of journalistic imagination and editorial or proprietorial agendas than to fact or research are ten a penny. The *Daily Mail*'s momentary posting earlier this month of an account of Amanda Knox's reaction ('sobbing uncontrollably') to the dismissal of her appeal against her murder conviction, when her appeal had in fact succeeded, is only the latest, slightly comical, episode in the ignoble history of British tabloid journalism. But I want to look at a bigger issue, the compensation culture which, as we all know, has come to blight our legal system and, through it, our society.

We know it because the press has repeatedly told us it is so. The expression seems to have originated in an article about welfare by Bernard Levin in *The Times* in 1993. Between 1996 and 2004, references to it in the press rose year on year from near-zero to over 450. It had some basis, without doubt, in the advent of conditional fee agreements and of claims management companies which were making a living by ambulance-chasing. But the House of Commons' Constitutional Affairs Committee in 2006 found no evidence that the growth of risk-aversion was related to these factors. Over the same period, although tribunal claims increased with the creation of new causes of action, the total number of claims in the courts steadily declined. Moreover, the great majority of awards that were made were small; and costs as a fraction of GDP, though in absolute terms embarrassingly high, were lower not only than in the US but than in much of Europe.[15]

This, naturally, had no effect at all on those for whom the existence of a compensation culture was a necessary condition for an assault on the Human Rights Act, the health and safety legislation, personal injury litigation and laws forbidding discrimination and restricting dismissal. The assault was supported—as it continues to be—by an unstoppable stream of news items about absurd claims, most of them allegedly human rights-based, showing how easy it now was to get compensation for anything. That few of them ever came to court, and that those which did generally failed, went pretty much unrecorded.

[15] See James Hand, 'The compensation culture: cliché or cause for concern?' (2010) 37 *Journal of Law and Society*.

The two spectres at this feast of fabrication have been the insurance industry, which foots most of the bills both for litigation and for settlements, and the press itself, for whom privacy claims have now joined the financial burden of libel actions. But there is a more serious agenda than the urge not to relinquish a good story whether it happens to be true or not. A significant proportion of compensation culture stories are attributed, usually falsely, to the Human Rights Act. Prisoners, the public now believes, can sue under the Act for not being allowed to vote or to access pornography; paedophiles and rapists can refuse on privacy grounds to register their electronic addresses and identities; robbers under siege by the police have to be supplied with Kentucky fried chicken and cigarettes; photographs of fugitive criminals cannot be publicised, because of their human rights; acquiring a cat is now a complete defence to deportation ... the nonsense rolls on, with very little to impede it.

In 2004 the Better Regulation Task Force subheaded their report on *Better Routes to Redress* 'Compensation culture: exploding the urban myth'. For they found that there was no such culture; what was causing problems was the belief that there was one. The report was welcomed by government and was acted on in the Compensation Act 2006, which regulated claims-management enterprises and restated the common law negligence test so as to protect desirable activities. But the flow of articles about the compensation culture actually peaked in the wake of the report, and it is still running at about 100 a year.

The report in 2006 of the Commons' Constitutional Affairs Committee, which I mentioned earlier, concluded, for the reasons I have touched on, that the UK was not moving towards, much less embedded in, a compensation culture. The problem, it found, was a culture of risk aversion which the myth was actually provoking. Enter a new government. The Prime Minister asked the veteran politician and entrepreneur Lord Young 'to investigate and report back ... on the rise of the compensation culture over the last decade, coupled with the current low standing that health and safety legislation now enjoys, and to suggest solutions'. Lawyers will admire the way the questions came armed with the answers: as every cross-examiner knows, you don't leave these things to chance.

Despite this, in his chapter captioned 'Compensation culture', Lord Young wrote:

> Britain's 'compensation culture' is fuelled by media stories ... and by constant adverts ... The problem of the compensation culture prevalent in society today is, however, one of perception rather than reality.

That, chiming as it did with all that had previously been established, seemed to be that.

But turn back to the title page of the report, and you read that it follows a review of 'the operation of health and safety laws and the growth of the compensation culture'. Then turn the page and read the Prime Minister's foreword:

> A damaging compensation culture has arisen …

If the health and safety legislation is to be cut back as an excessive burden on employers and their insurers, and the legal aid system as an excessive burden on the Treasury, the myth that these, along with the Human Rights Act, are fuelling a culture of extravagant claims and personal irresponsibility is too useful to shelve simply because it isn't true.

I have written elsewhere about the absence from the texts of the world's human rights instruments of a right to be told the truth, or at least a right not to be lied to. As the philosopher Julian Baggini recently pointed out, Winston Smith in the nightmare state of *1984* was not asking for the luxury of freedom to believe and to assert that two and two make five: the freedom he wanted was simply to be able to insist, in a society which had lost its grip on truth, that two and two make four. We have not yet come to that pass, but the steady and serious erosion of the bright line between knowledge and belief is mirrored, in the world of journalism and of politics, in the now routine collapsing of fact into comment, and of belief into fact.

If, then, the right of free expression is capable of being a stalking horse for the power to mislead and to disinform, where do we stand? There is no easy answer. I have said both in and out of court that the one thing that would be even worse is a ministry of truth—a body empowered to decide officially what is fact and what is not. But, as I have also argued elsewhere, the marketplace of ideas in which the true drives out the false is a fiction which no thinking survivor of the twentieth century—the century of the grand and murderous lie—can possibly believe in. Somewhere between the unacceptable—a ministry of truth—and the unbelievable—the marketplace of ideas—an answer has to be found. Patently, in 2011, it is not self-regulation. In the not too distant future Lord Justice Leveson may tell us what it is.

6

The North American Meetings: A Canadian Perspective

BRYAN FINLAY QC

Bryan Finlay QC is recognised as one of the top litigation lawyers in Canada. He is Partner Emeritus at the Toronto law firm WeirFoulds LLP. Bryan has been an Honorary Overseas Member of COMBAR for many years and has been a regular attendee at the annual North American meetings both sides of the Atlantic.

THE NORTH AMERICAN meetings have been a great success. The substantive content covers the whole range of trans-border legal issues, with contributions coming from members from the United States, Bermuda, West Indies, Canada and England. However, I do not wish to concentrate on these matters in this short chapter; rather I wish to focus on what makes the North American meetings unique and occasions we look forward to year after year.

The most striking aspect of COMBAR is its collegiality. The North American meetings may at their most comprise no more than about 75 members, about one-half of whom are from the western hemisphere. It is, however, the English Bar that imprints its personality on the occasion. This is not surprising. After all it is an English organisation. And it is that personality that I would suggest brings most of us non-English lawyers back again and again. I will try to describe the COMBAR personality as viewed by this Canadian member. First, of course, COMBAR cannot escape its membership: litigation lawyers: that odd group of men and women who devote themselves to excessively hard work only to see it, on more occasions than we would like to admit, go to pieces in front of our very eyes. For this group, a few days away with spouses, partners and children is a time to be treasured. Then there is the English sense of humour that infects almost every aspect of the meetings. This presents itself at times in almost a Wodehousian sense. Into this mix, stir the intellectual and professional ruminations of the members, and behold the product: an enjoyable, interesting and rewarding event. In short, an occasion of great collegiality. And, as an aside, a collegiality that has led to numerous retainers.

The Locations

The sites of the meetings are chosen only after consultation with the members. They are with rare exception of a high calibre. Understandably, some stand out more than others, and each member will have favourites. For me, Berlin stands out as one of the best.

We will not forget the dinner atop of the Reichstag where a German lawyer gave the after dinner speech on a topic something like 'Humour in German Fraud'. In a city of ghosts (as described by Jeff Leon), the choice of topic was odd.

However, all that disappeared into insignificance when we were confronted with Stephen Moriarty QC in his cycling regalia. The English Bar may be well acquainted with this apparition, but it hit us as if we had stepped back in time to before the last war (that's WWII). We had joined up with Stephen, Clare and Veronica for a bicycle tour. Stephen's outfit was certainly of a pre-war, if not earlier, design: a combination of plus fours, tweed, with expansion flaps, various toggles and straps, and pockets and receptacles in abundance for various objects. Finally, while I could not tell for sure, I was almost certain that, in case we were caught behind enemy lines, it had a silk map of Eastern Europe stitched into it somewhere and that the buttons either concealed compasses or could be eaten, or both. While we thought that this could not possibly be standard wear, we were assured that Stephen wore it into London each day as he cycled into work.

One of the rare exceptions where the location left something to be desired was the meeting in Boston. Our hotel, which had seen better days, seemed to be serviced by taxi cabs operated only by Russians, whose driving focused on running red lights at great speed and driving down sidewalks.

The Programmes

The quality of the presentation is generally most impressive. The organising committee wrestles with the question of demonstrations or moots. Do they work? How could they be improved? This I don't think is unusual. Demonstrations or moots have the tendency to develop a life all of their own, especially where you have the level of thespian talent that the English Bar demonstrates. For example, who will forget the expert witness played by Charles Béar QC being cross-examined? It could have been a piece from 'Beyond the Fringe'.

I have participated in my share of the moots. My first experience with COMBAR was in Toronto as counsel in a moot opposite Robin Knowles CBE, QC with John Sopinka presiding. I thought at the time that if this was the standard of the moot (present company excluded), it was a most impressive organisation indeed. Perhaps the one that stands out the most memorably is where Nikki Singla, Kannon Shanmugam and I faced off on one side against three formidable opponents whose names have dissolved in the mists of time. It was not the actual moot that was memorable, rather it was waiting for Nikki to show up in Boston. I thought it would be important for the three of us to meet beforehand to go over our notes. Nikki's plane seemed to arrive at the same time as the moot commenced. I have come to understand since that this may simply be a characteristic of the English Bar.

There is always at the meetings an honoured guest: almost always a Justice from the Commercial Court in London. Their attendance adds a certain 'authority' to our gatherings, and they can always be counted on for a few insightful remarks on some topic of general interest. The only one, whom I can remember, who completely lost the American/Canadian audience was the Justice who, in his after dinner speech, spoke about a case involving corruption in cricket, describing the case using only cricket terms.

But one cannot leave a discussion about the programmes without mentioning 'the table' at the meetings. It may be my imagination but 'the table' seems to have grown over the years to now resemble what must have been used at the Peace Conference in Versailles. We look across at each other with a sense of self-importance befitting our surroundings.

I can only believe it was the surroundings that infused the members with feelings of self-importance that caused the moot in Prague to hold me in contempt and to award costs against me personally for failing to appear. (We were turned back in Toronto at the Air Canada check-in counter for not having a visa). An award of costs, I might add, that is still mentioned by some honourable members to this day in a threatening sort of way.

Veronica

No chapter on COMBAR would be complete without mentioning Veronica. She is to COMBAR what Jeeves is to Bertie Wooster. What a treasure! She makes the whole thing run with a charm and effortlessness that is a privilege to behold. Through her, we have dined in and visited the most wonderful places, following in the footsteps of the rich and famous. What is more, she likes to cycle with Stephen and Clare.

Friendships

This is where I wish to end my remarks. I started off with collegiality, but friendships are more than simple collegiality. We are very fortunate to have made good friends, both amongst the English and the honorary members. And I am sure this is true for many members. Strange it is that COMBAR has been the vehicle that has even furthered friendships with our fellow Canadians. We owe that to the spirit that is COMBAR.

7

Advocacy in the Commercial Court

THE HON MR JUSTICE TEARE

The Hon Mr Justice Teare gave this talk to COMBAR members as part of the Professional Education series of talks back in March 2012. It took place at the Royal College of Surgeons, Lincoln's Inn.

LAST WEEK WAS a normal week in the Commercial Court. I received a 100-page skeleton argument in support of continuing an injunction and opposing a challenge to the jurisdiction; in another application challenging the jurisdiction I had received skeleton arguments amounting in total to over 110 pages from one side, and 117 pages from the other side. And for the closing written submissions in an action, I received 156 pages for one side and 175 for the other side, the latter being complemented by 980 footnotes.

An impartial observer might well conclude from that, that oral advocacy has a very limited role in the modern Commercial Court.

But despite the production of such lengthy examples of written advocacy, the tradition of oral advocacy in the Commercial Court, as indeed in all our courts, remains strong. But the advocate requires skill at both oral and written advocacy and so I shall say something about both.

The skeleton argument is the first piece of advocacy to which the judge is exposed in a case.

Written skeleton arguments were first introduced in the Commercial Court and the Court of Appeal by Lord Donaldson in the 1980s. Since then, they have become an established practice in almost every field of law. But we are a long way from the American and European practice of severely limiting oral argument to very short periods of time. I regard oral argument, in common I think with many other judges (though not perhaps all), as a valuable way of identifying the right answer to a case. In particular, it enables the judge to put to the advocate the points in a case which are troubling him, and gives the advocate the opportunity of persuading the judge that those points are not the obstacles the judge thinks they are or might be. However, there are pressures on court time, and so written skeleton arguments are a cost-effective way of explaining the nature of the case, identifying the issues, summarising the most material facts and the relevant law, and explaining the remedy which the advocate is seeking. If the judge has read and digested each side's skeleton argument, there should be no need for any detailed opening in a trial, save perhaps ensuring that the judge is familiar with the most important documents in the case.

It was never intended that skeleton arguments should be like written briefs in the American courts, which, to a large extent, take the place of oral advocacy. That is not the English tradition. And the Commercial Court Guide urges you to be concise and to avoid arguing the case at length. However, as the length of documents which I mentioned earlier suggests, there is a marked tendency towards providing written briefs on the part of counsel, which the courts seek to discourage. Could I remind you of three judicial comments in the last year or so.

Lord Justice Mummery said this about skeleton arguments in the Court of Appeal.

1. We remind practitioners that skeleton arguments should not be prepared as verbatim scripts to be read out in public or as footnoted theses to be read in private. Good skeleton arguments are tools with practical uses: an agenda for the hearing, a summary of the main points, propositions and arguments to be developed orally, a useful way of noting citations and references, a convenient place for making cross references, a time-saving means of avoiding unnecessary dictation to the court and laborious and pointless note-taking by the court.
2. Skeleton arguments are aids to oral advocacy. They are not written briefs which are used in some jurisdictions as substitutes for oral advocacy. An unintended and unfortunate side effect of the growth in written advocacy (written opening and closing submissions and 'speaking notes', as well as skeleton arguments) has been that too many practitioners, at increased cost to their clients and diminishing assistance to the court, burden their opponents and the court with written briefs. They are anything but brief. The result is that there is no real saving of legal costs, or of precious hearing, reading and writing time. As has happened in this case, the opponent's skeleton argument becomes longer and the judgment reflecting the lengthy written submissions tends to be longer than is really necessary to explain to the parties why they have won or lost an appeal.
3. The skeletal nature of written advocacy is in danger of being overlooked. In some cases we are weighed down by the skeleton arguments and when we dare to complain about the time they take up, we are sometimes told that we can read them 'in our own time' after the hearing. In our judgment, this is not what appellate advocacy is about, or ought to be about, in this court.[1]

Lord Justice Toulson referred in a judgment to a skeleton argument 'which was a grotesque example of a tendency to overburden the court with documents of grossly disproportionate quantity and length'.[2]

[1] *Tombstone Ltd v Raja* [2008] EWCA Civ 1444; [2009] 1 WLR 1143.
[2] *Midgulf International Ltd v Groupe Chimique Tunisien* [2010] EWCA (Civ) 66.

And Sir Anthony May, the then President of the Queen's Bench Division, warned that if counsel provide excessive written briefs rather than true skeleton arguments, the costs may be disallowed or the time for oral submissions may be curtailed.[3]

I recognise that these statements, though clear and unambiguous in their tone and content, present a difficulty for the advocate. Skeleton arguments, particularly at first instance, tend to have two functions to perform. First, they are skeleton arguments in the original sense of a brief introduction to the case and the issues, which saves time in oral openings. But secondly they provide assistance to the judge when writing his judgment. This second function is increasingly common. Witness statements are now almost always taken as the witness's evidence-in-chief. The judge has to read them before the witness is called, but inevitably he cannot take in all the fine detail. Only parts of them may be subject to cross-examination and so receive attention during the trial. In the old days, cases proceeded at the pace at which a judge could absorb the evidence and think about it. Today, trials proceed at a much faster pace. There is usually much thinking to be done after a hearing is over. Those parts of a skeleton argument which set out a chronology of the relevant events with references to the detailed evidence are therefore often of great assistance. The same goes for expositions on the law with references to the authorities. And perhaps for detailed argument. But all such material means that skeleton arguments tend to become unwieldy documents, which is contrary to their original purpose. Perhaps the best way of resolving the tension between these two uses of the modern skeleton argument is to prepare the skeleton argument in a form in which there are two parts. The first is the skeleton argument in the short form originally envisaged by Lord Donaldson, desired by Lord Justice Mummery and required by the Commercial Court Guide. The second is an annex which sets out the detailed and cross-referenced chronology and exposition of the law, into which the judge can dip as required, during and after the hearing. Since the judge is the consumer of the skeleton argument, it is essential that it be judge-friendly and in a form which he finds helpful and not tiresome. Anyone drafting a skeleton argument should envisage the judge coming out of court at about 4.15 or 4.30 pm after struggling with a difficult case and, perhaps, with advocates anxious to ensure that he understands every detail of that difficult case. He gets back to his room and there on his desk are several boxes of lever arch files topped of by two thick and indexed skeleton arguments. He feels very weary and wonders how on earth he is going to find the time or the energy to read sufficient of the case before 10.30 am the next day. If the next day is a Friday summons day, he may have skeleton argument in four or five cases. It is therefore essential that

[3] *Khadez v Asiz* [2010] EWCA 716.

the skeleton argument should, at the very least, contain a short and simple introduction to the case. Anything too complex will only elicit a judicial groan. The motto must be: 'keep it simple'. By all means have appendices of useful material which the judge can peruse at a later stage, but do not ignore the simple introduction to the case and to the issues which will arise. Always be mindful of keeping the judge on your side. Do not antagonise him by detail which at first sight appears impenetrable.

The listing office does pay attention to the estimated reading time, but there is rarely enough time in the judicial day to allot those numbers of hours suggested by counsel. A Commercial Court judge is not just judging your case. He has judgments in other cases to write, he has paper applications to consider and, like every Queen's Bench judge, he has paper applications for leave to appeal in criminal cases to consider. In addition he may have a role in the administration of the courts, which eats into his time.

Estimates of reading time are very often underestimates. That is often because too much is put in the reading list. So what should be in them?

Be merciful. Never ask the judge to read the pleadings. By the time of hearing, they should have served their purpose. If the skeleton is for an interlocutory hearing, the judge should have the benefit of the case memorandum. If the skeleton is for a trial, you will have summarised the issues which arise on the pleadings and which remain in issue in the skeleton.

Documents

It is only necessary to ask the judge to read those documents which are truly essential to assist him in understanding the issues. It is quite unnecessary to ask the judge to read those which witnesses are going to be taken through in cross examination. Yet many detailed documents are often put on the list, quite unnecessarily.

Witness Statements

If possible, summarise what is agreed, and ask the judge to read only those parts of the evidence which remain in issue. This is particularly necessary these days, when witness statements tend to be a vehicle for stating the entirety of a party's case, complete with comments on, and explanations of, a great many documents. Point out when witnesses are due to be called so that the judge can stage the reading of witness statements throughout the trial. What is the purpose of asking the judge to read all the statements in a case before the start of the trial? It may be a week or more before some witnesses are called.

Expert's Reports

It is rarely, if ever, necessary to invite the court to read the entirety of the expert's reports—yet counsel often do. I usually content myself with the expert's memorandum of what is agreed and what is not agreed—and then go to the summary of the experts' opinions at the end of their report. If it is really necessary for the judge to read the detail of the reports, the reading list should be carefully constructed around what is in issue, identifying those parts which of the report which relate to each issue.

I recognise that this requires more work on the advocate's part than simply listing everything, but it will enable the judge to read and concentrate on what truly matters. Which must, or at any rate ought to be, to the advocate's advantage.

Oral Advocacy

What appeals must often depend on the individual judge; I can only speak for myself—you will develop your own views as to what appeals to judge A and what appeals to judge B, and you must tailor your oral address accordingly. The task of an advocate is to persuade—but of course only by fair means, not foul.

May I just dwell on that for a moment? The Bar Council's Code of Conduct makes clear that the advocate's overriding duty is to the court:

> to act with independence in the interests of justice: he must assist the Court in the administration of justice and must not deceive or knowingly or recklessly mislead the Court.

Why is the advocate's overriding duty to the court? It is because the court and the advocate have a common interest in the administration of justice. The judge relies upon the advocate in this regard and trusts him. Without that reliance and trust, the administration of justice would be less fair and less effective.

This duty was emphasised by Lord Neuberger, the Master of the Rolls, at the Bar Conference in 2010. Speaking of the advocate's duties he said:

> they are all duties which require the consumer interest to take second place to the public interest. It should also be said those duties not only flow from our commitment to the public interest, but equally from our commitment to the constitutional principle of the rule of law. The rule of law would be little more than a phrase for idle moments, if lawyers—in the interests of the consumer—acted as if anything goes. The rule of law is a rule of integrity. It supports the foundations of our society, without which reference to the consumer interest would be utterly empty of content and meaning.

> … without the rule of law and a robustly independent legal profession committed to its core values and the public interest we would have no civil society.'

Now let me return to the practicalities of oral advocacy. How should your oral address relate to the skeleton argument—are you following the skeleton argument or ignoring it?

There is no rule about this. It is a matter for your judgment which you think more effective in the particular case. But whichever you decide to do, tell the judge.

- It is irksome for the judge trying to find the point being made by counsel orally in his skeleton argument only to be told, when the judge asks, that it is not there.
- Similarly if the point is in the skeleton argument, it is helpful to know that, because the judge need not then take a full note; I often add manuscript notes on the skeleton argument.
- Should you read the skeleton argument? Usually not; it is very boring and the impartial observer would be astonished to realise that a document which the judge has already been asked to read (and probably has read) is now being solemnly read out to him.
- If you are going to read it, tell the judge and ask him whether he would find it helpful—if he has not had time to take it on board (as you suspect may be the case), he might well say it is.
- But even if you do read it, it is better to emphasise what you regard to be the best points, and what you wish the judge to concentrate on—if he has not read the others, he will do so before writing his judgment.
- That makes it more interesting for the judge, which makes it more likely that you will persuade him.

Whatever you plan to do, you must be flexible—because the judge may not have had time to read, let alone digest, the skeleton arguments. The advocate therefore has to be ready for the judge who has read and understood everything; the judge who has been so pressed that he has only glanced at the skeleton arguments; and the judge who has dipped into some passages but not all, and may perhaps have a distorted view of the case. The appropriate opening will differ for each of those judges.

Should you assume the judge has the relevant facts in mind and has understood them?

- My advice is never assume that the judge has in mind all the facts that you, who have lived with the case for days, weeks or even months, have fully in mind. I am always surprised by what counsel think I have absorbed, or ought to have absorbed, from pre-reading.
- Even though you have given the judge a chronology and asked him to read the witness statements factual, it is unsafe to assume that the judge has taken it all on board.

— So take the judge to the essential facts of the case, even though they may be obvious to you and set out in the skeleton argument—if the judge has them in mind and thinks what you are doing is unnecessary, he will tell you.

This applies both to applications and trials, but particularly to applications—when a judge has read, hurriedly, the skeleton arguments in four or five applications between say 3.00 pm and 7.00 pm the day before, and before 10.30 am the following morning, it is impossible (at any rate for me) to have instant recollection of the facts of each case throughout the Friday.

— For trials, the judge will have had more time to read; but nevertheless, the judge has had little time compared with what you have had; and an urgent application for a freezing order may, unexpectedly, have taken up much of his reading time in any event.
— Much the same applies to documents—no doubt they were on the reading list; but still take the judge to them and point out the important passages—if the judge already knows and understands them, he will tell you.

Make simple and concise submissions. Why should you do so? Because they will be much easier for the judge to take on board. Of course more work is required to produce a short and simple submission than a longer, rambling one, but the time is well spent and the product is much more likely to persuade the judge.

Remember the wise words of Lord Bingham: you should concentrate on 'winnowing out the essential and crucial from the inessential and peripheral'—

> to distil the point that really matters is greatly to strengthen the effectiveness of the argument. That is after all the stock in trade of the outstanding advocate.

If a point has to be developed because is it in truth a complex point. it can of course be developed—but it is easier for the judge to understand the development of the point if he has first understood the basic point on which you are relying.

When should you seek to demolish the argument of your opponent? You will have your own views on this, but my advice is:

— Concentrate on your own argument.
— Never assume that the judge has understood your case merely because you have asked him to read it.
— You have your answers to your opponent's case and you may be very anxious to tell the judge what they are; but it is surely essential for the judge to understand your own case first.
— If you are the claimant, you will have a right of reply and the last word. You lose nothing by saving your response to your opponent's argument

until your reply; indeed the force of a response is often all the greater if the judge has already been persuaded by the defendant that he might be right.

— If you are the defendant, you will have to reply to the claimants' points, but do so after you have set out your own case with clarity.

What use should you make of adjectives and adverbs? My advice is not to use either.

When dealing with your opponent's argument, give the judge *reasons* for rejecting it; it is not persuasive to denigrate it by describing it as hopeless, completely hopeless or utterly hopeless, any more than it is persuasive to describe your own argument as plainly right. I am instinctively on my guard when an advocate makes excessive use of adjectives; if he has a good case, they are unnecessary; I am persuaded by reasoning, not by abuse. If it is appropriate to use adjectives—and it sometimes is—remember Lord Bingham's advice:

> The effective advocate is not usually he or she who stigmatises conduct as disgraceful, outrageous or monstrous but the advocate who describes it as surprising, regrettable or disappointing.

Authorities

I have observed at least two different approaches.

1. One is to take the judge to the passage in the authority which sets out the principle relied upon without explaining how the issue arose in that case in order to see it in context.
2. The other is to summarise the facts, the issues and the decision—and then refer to the statement of principle which led to that decision.

I find the first approach unhelpful—without knowing the context in which a statement of principle was made, I will not be persuaded that the statement of principle, however clearly expressed, is applicable to the case I am deciding; in law, context is all

If I am merely referred to the statement of principle, I will have to study its context myself; surely the advocate should tackle that, to ensure the judge gets the right end of the stick. These days, when so many cases are cited which are not reported in the law reports but are found on Bailii without a headnote, is it particularly necessary for the advocate to put the statement of principle in context.

In argument, you must engage with the judge. I often put to counsel what I think may be the answer to a case in order to see what, if anything, there can be said against it. That is the great advantage of oral argument. Some counsel, admittedly few in the Commercial Court, do not appear to recognise that I am inviting a reply, and think that it is my final and concluded view and meekly say 'Well, if that is the way your lordship sees it, there is nothing to add.' But it is essential, for a just resolution to a case, that where the judge makes a comment or advances a view with which counsel disagrees, he or she robustly, but politely, advances the contrary view. I am grateful when counsel tells me I am wrong, and why. Whether or not I am wrong, the opposing arguments are then clearly delineated—and I can go away and decide what I think the right answer is.

Closing Submissions at the End of a Trial

In substantial cases, closing submissions are often put in writing and sometimes there is a short adjournment for them to be prepared and for the judge to read them. Oral closings will usually in those circumstances be given a limited amount of time. Some suggest they are unnecessary because the judge has the benefit of full written submissions. But, as I said earlier in this talk, I find oral argument at the end of a trial helpful because I can seek answers to what I consider to be difficult points. But apart from being prepared to answer questions from the judge on any part of the case, what should counsel plan to say on such occasions? There is no time to read out the written submissions, and in any event that would be absurd. Nor is anything to be gained by hurriedly mentioning as many of the topics covered in writing as can be mentioned in the time available. In my view, the advocate has to concentrate on what he considers to be the point or points most likely to win the case, and make sure the judge has them well in mind. If his opponent has a point which the advocate considers particularly dangerous, he may also wish to make sure the judge has in mind the reasons why that point is wrong. What those points are requires an exercise of judgment by the advocate. Lord Donaldson used to say that there was only one point in every case. The difficulty, of course, is to decide what that point is. It is an occasion when the advocate has the opportunity to display his judgment and his skill.

In conclusion, whether you are preparing oral or written submissions, I urge you to heed Lord Neuberger's advice:

> A skilled advocate follows George Orwell's rules: they never use a long word where a short one will do; wherever it is possible to cut a word out, they always cut it out. Their submissions are well prepared. They know their brief. They know which points have merit. They concede where concession is proper.

Finally, let me finish by mentioning an exchange in court which perhaps illustrates the respect which the Bench and the Bar have for each other, and the easy manner in which they can and should address each other in court. A circuit judge, HH Judge Dean, was hearing his last case, and before commencing his last summing-up he wished to mark the occasion by thanking the Bar for their assistance over a great number of years. In particular he wished to thank the counsel before him that day, who had appeared before him in a great many cases and whom he knew very well: Mr Smith for the prosecution, and Mr ... At that point the judge's memory went a complete blank and he could not remember the name of defence counsel. The silence grew longer but the judge could not remember counsel's name. It was eventually broken by defence counsel getting to his feet and saying. 'The name is Spittal. And if it assists, your Honour's name is Dean.'

8

The Somewhat Uncommon Law of Commerce

THE HONOURABLE THE CHIEF JUSTICE SUNDARESH MENON*

The Honourable the Chief Justice Sundaresh Menon delivered the Annual COMBAR Lecture in November 2013 at Lincoln's Inn Old Hall. Sundaresh Menon is the Chief Justice of Singapore and a former Attorney-General of Singapore. He is the first ethnic Indian to hold those posts.

IT GIVES ME great pleasure to be here at Lincoln's Inn to deliver this year's COMBAR lecture. As lawyers, we hold membership not just of our own legal systems; we belong also to a global fraternity, and it is in this spirit that I take up this evening's subject. It is a subject which is close to the hearts of both our legal communities, situated as we are in the financial centres of Europe on the one hand and South East Asia on the other. At the same time it is also in the sphere of commerce that the dualism between an international outlook and a domestic rootedness is perhaps at its most visceral. How we choose to structure and propagate our laws of commerce can have an impact on the calculus of economic actors and, consequently, on the behaviour of the markets they transact in.

In the age of globalisation this impact has been magnified in both scale and reach. So our subject this evening is not just theoretical—it also impinges on the business end of the law. This is where the law is converted into hard currency, into goods shifting across borders—and, of course, into more or less work for lawyers. To adopt the deliberately broad definition of the foremost thinker about commercial law, Professor Roy Goode, commercial law is that branch of law which is concerned with rights and duties arising from the supply of goods and services in the way of trade.[1]

In looking at this varied area of the law I do not propose to stray from its core source and subject, which is the law of contract. To borrow again from Professor Goode, whose elegant summation cannot be bettered: 'commercial law draws for its sustenance on all the great streams of law that together

* I am very grateful to my law clerk, Mr Jonathan Yap, for his considerable assistance in the research and preparation of this lecture.

[1] Ewan Mckendrick, *Goode on Commercial Law*, 4th edn (London, LexisNexis, 2009) 8.

make up the corpus of English jurisprudence, with the law of contract as its core, while equity acts now as its handmaiden, now as the keeper of its conscience'.[2] Contract law is so foundational to commercial law simply because contracts are essential to commerce. Without the certainty or, at least, the security provided by a contract, modern-day commerce would not be possible. But how is the understanding of this security likely to differ as borders are crossed?

Though our laws and our legal systems share a common heritage—indeed, ours is the progeny of the English system—there are nonetheless divergences in the substance of commercial law between our jurisdictions. It is perhaps no longer surprising that the common law is not quite common after all. What is interesting about some of these divergences though, is their source. To a greater or lesser degree, the influence of European civil law has resulted in the development of new ideas in the English common law.

One would expect that such divergences might come at an economic cost. Heterogeneity in commercial law creates friction in the movement of goods and businesses across borders, and seems to swim against the tide of increasing economic integration which has been the story of the post-Cold War world.[3]

I propose this evening to draw out just a few illustrative divergences and then place them within context, so that we might critically evaluate whether this is a problem going forward. More specifically, we might ask whether this is a problem which needs a solution, and what such a solution might look like.

I will examine three specific areas of contract law where Singapore has diverged from England—the interpretation and implication of contract terms, remoteness of damage, and the duty to act in good faith. In each of these areas, the Singapore courts have felt the tension between our own legal experience and the weight of English case law. As will become evident, there are important differences, but also interesting similarities between us.

Setting the Context

I would like to preface the discussion with a brief survey of Singapore's current legal system. Since the passage of the Application of English Law Act in 1993, it has been clear that while English common law continues to have weight and influence in Singapore, this is only so far as it is applicable to the circumstances of Singapore, and subject to such modifications as those circumstances may require.[4] In the same year, Singapore abolished all appeals

[2] RM Goode, *Commercial Law in the Next Millennium* (London, Sweet & Maxwell, 1998) 8–9.

[3] One of the more prominent mainstream accounts being Thomas L Friedman, *The Lexus and the Olive Tree* (London, Harper Collins, 1999).

[4] Application of English Law Act (Cap 7A, 1994 Rev Ed), s 3.

to the Privy Council[5] and Parliament passed a legislative amendment to constitute a permanent Court of Appeal.[6]

From today's vantage point, I think it is fair to say that although the Singapore legal system continues to have an umbilical relationship with English law, we are growing up on our own terms.[7] English law continues to carry persuasive weight and remains extensively cited in our courts;[8] on the other hand, there are encouraging signs that our own case law is forming a critical mass.[9] Indeed, the emergence of a distinctively *Singaporean* law of contract can be taken as a bellwether of our progress, this being an area of law where received English authorities were previously taken as cardinal.[10] The principal mode of this evening's lecture will consist of looking at what one of our leading textbooks terms the autochthonous law of contract in Singapore.[11]

While Singapore law has been working through its adolescence, English commercial law has been increasingly shaped by the UK's membership of the European Union. The Treaty of Rome which created the European Economic Community was conceived for the express purpose of achieving economic integration through the creation of a common market.[12] This project reached a watershed with the creation of a monetary union by the Maastricht Treaty and has since been further galvanised by the entry into force of the Lisbon Treaty. Despite some recent troubles, the European Union, as it stands today, is the pre-eminent model of regional integration in the global economic order. The work of European legislators has been buttressed by a monumental effort at legal harmonisation led by the European Court of Justice in such early landmark cases as *Costa v ENEL*[13] and *Van Gend en Loos.*[14] Following the passage of the European Communities Act in 1972, and the decision of the House of Lords in the *Factortame* case of 1990,[15] EU law is now part of the body of commercial law which English courts will have reference to. Under these conditions there can be little room for doubt that English commercial law will gradually take on a more European

[5] Constitution of the Republic of Singapore (Amendment) Act 1993 (Act 17 of 1993).

[6] Supreme Court of Judicature (Amendment) Act 1993 (Act 16 of 1993).

[7] See, in this regard, GW Bartholomew, 'The Singapore Legal System' in R Hassan (ed), *Singapore: Society in Transition* (Oxford, Oxford University Press, 1976) 97–109.

[8] See Andrew Phang Boon Leong et al, *The Law of Contract in Singapore* (Singapore, Academy Publishing, 2012) paras 02.076–02.077.

[9] Y Goh and P Tan, 'An Empirical Study on the Development of Singapore Law' (2011) 23 *Singapore Academy of Law Journal* 176, 215.

[10] Chan, *An Introduction to the Singapore Legal System* (Singapore, Malayan Law Journal, 1986) 9–10; Phang (1986) 28 *Malaya Law Review* 242, 252–56.

[11] See n 8, paras 02.073–02.080.

[12] Treaty establishing the European Economic Community, Art 100A.

[13] *Costa v ENEL* [1964] ECR 585.

[14] *Van Gend en Loos* [1963] ECR 1.

[15] *R v Secretary of State for Transport ex p Factortame Ltd and others* [1991] AC 603, esp [4] (Lord Bridge of Harwich).

complexion,[16] even as London maintains its importance as the preferred venue for international litigation.[17]

The first shades of a similar process are also beginning to emerge in Singapore, with a discernible increase in the number of international litigants coming through our courts. Singapore is also at the forefront of the drive to create an ASEAN Economic Community in 2015, a substantial project that remains on track for completion. Just last month the Prime Minister of India pledged to sign a free trade agreement on services and investment with the ASEAN bloc. This will deepen economic ties between ASEAN and India, and is expected to boost bilateral trade to US$100 billion within two years. The surge of economic expansion has been supported by legal change as well. Singapore is leading the ASEAN Integration Through Law Project, which seeks to advance the community-building aims of ASEAN through the development of a collective framework of both substantive and procedural legal principles.[18] This is an exciting project, and perhaps there will come a day when we can speak of a 'Southeast Asian' commercial law in the way one might speak of European commercial law.

I do not mean to gaze into the crystal ball. It suffices for present purposes to say that as two separate but similar systems of law in very different parts of the world, Singapore and London are on parallel trajectories. This presents an opportunity for both comparison and commentary, which may yet have some resonance with the harmonisation of commercial law on a grander scale.

The Interpretation and Implication of Contract Terms

Interpretation

The law on the interpretation and implication of contract terms in Singapore is set out in a trilogy of decisions from the Court of Appeal. The first case, *Zurich Insurance*,[19] substantively adopted Lord Hoffmann's celebrated restatement in *Investors' Compensation Scheme*[20] as the appropriate approach to contractual interpretation in Singapore. *Zurich Insurance* was

[16] For a more general and abstract analysis, see John Merryman, 'On the Convergence (and Divergence) of the Civil Law and the Common Law' (1981) 17 *Stanford Journal of International Law* 357.

[17] www.thelawyer.com/news/practice-areas/litigation-news/international-litigants-in-london-rise-by-a-third-in-three-years/3004520.article.

[18] *Integration through Law; The ASEAN Way in a Comparative Context—Mission Statement* (Revised 25 April 2011) 2–3.

[19] *Zurich Insurance (Singapore) Pte Ltd v B-Gold Interior Design & Construction Pte Ltd* [2008] 3 SLR(R) 1029.

[20] *Investors Compensation Scheme Ltd v West Bromwich Building Society* [1998] 1 WLR 896, 912–13.

a case which concerned the issue of whether fire damage was covered by the terms of an insurance policy, but to reach an answer, our apex court had to map out a significant expanse of contract law. The principal result of this endeavour was an affirmation of the contextual approach to contractual interpretation. In the course of doing so the court also found that the parol evidence rule continued to persist in section 94 of the Evidence Act (Cap 97, 1990 Rev Ed), which states that no evidence of an oral agreement shall be admitted as between parties to any agreement which has been reduced into writing for the purpose of varying, adding to, or subtracting from its terms. *Zurich Insurance* also provides valuable guidance[21] on what extrinsic evidence may be admissible to aid in the contextual interpretation of the contract; specifically, it must be evidence which is relevant, reasonably available to all contracting parties and which relates to a clear and obvious context. One might view this as very much aligned with the prevailing approach to contractual interpretation in the wider Commonwealth, and also generally faithful to the English common law.

To that extent, *Zurich Insurance* serves as a useful example to show that where English law has moved in a direction which accords with our judgment of logic, fairness, and commercial soundness, we have converged even if we were to recognise that the original impetus for such a shift might not be of direct relevance to Singapore. In delivering the judgment of the court, VK Rajah JA noted[22] that the contextual approach might be perceived as a symptom of the Europeanisation of the English common law. Regardless of this characterisation, to which I shall return later in this lecture, there remains a happy coincidence between Singapore and English contract law on this issue. In *Zurich Insurance* Rajah JA attributed the success of the contextual approach to its accordance with ordinary commerce, and noted that when 'faced with a wealth of text but a dearth of context, [the courts] have often attributed to contracting parties artificial objective intentions that are divorced from reality.'[23] I would echo these sentiments and add that ultimately, the collective shift towards contextualism has been motivated by the desire to do commercial justice by the contracting parties. Contracts are meant to embody agreements, not embalm them. The commercial realities which animated the entry into a contract ought not to be lost on account of the inert—and inevitably imprecise—words used to evidence it. At the same time, however, it is important that in the attempt to contextualise the written contract so as to ascertain the parties' objective agreement, we do not upset the commercial certainty which written contracts are meant to engender. This is a point which, as we will see later, I have taken up in a recent decision.

[21] See n 19, [132].
[22] ibid [133].
[23] ibid.

Implication

In the second case, *Foo Jong Peng*,[24] the Singapore Court of Appeal had occasion to examine the implication of contract terms. The case concerned the question of whether the rules of a Chinese clan association contained an implied term permitting the management committee to remove its members before the expiry of their term of office. The Court was invited, in particular, to consider the decision of the Privy Council in *AG v Belize*,[25] which arguably stood for the novel proposition that the implication of contract terms is simply an exercise in the interpretation of the contract as a whole. Lord Hoffmann, in giving the advice of the Privy Council, was characteristically bold in his exposition:[26]

> in every case in which it is said that some provision ought to be implied in an instrument, the question for the court is whether such a provision would spell out in express words what the instrument, read against the relevant background, would reasonably be understood to mean ... There is only one question: is that what the instrument, read as a whole against the relevant background, would reasonably be understood to mean?

The common—but by no means *only*—view is that by this reformulation of the doctrine of terms implied in fact, Lord Hoffman effected, at one and the same time, the cannibalisation of implication by interpretation and the replacement of the time-honoured 'business efficacy' and 'officious bystander' tests.[27]

Insofar as this appraisal of Lord Hoffmann's advice is accurate, the Singapore Court of Appeal declined to follow *Belize*. Affirming the observations of the Court in an earlier decision, the Court held in *Foo Jong Peng* that such a reformulation would result in a lack of concrete rules as well as in practical uncertainty. Further, Andrew Phang JA's judgment concluded that there were sound reasons underlying the received taxonomy of interpretation and implication, besides the 'officious bystander' and 'business efficacy' tests:[28]

> In summary, although the process of the implication of terms does involve the concept of interpretation, it entails a *specific form or conception of interpretation* which is *separate and distinct from the more general* process of interpretation (in particular, interpretation of the express terms of a particular document). Indeed, the process of the implication of terms *necessarily* involves a situation where it is

[24] *Foo Jong Peng and others v Phua Kiah Mai and another* [2012] 4 SLR 1267.

[25] *AG of Belize v Belize Telecom Ltd* [2009] 1 WLR 1988.

[26] ibid [21].

[27] See Paul S Davies, 'Recent Developments in the Law of Implied Terms' [2010] *Lloyd's Maritime and Commercial Law Quarterly* 140; *Crema v Cenkos Securities plc* [2011] 1 WLR 2066 [37]–[39]; *Chantry Estates v Anderson* [2010] EWCA Civ 314 [14]–[16], all cited in *Sembcorp* [77] (see n 37).

[28] See n 25, [36].

> precisely because the *express* term(s) are *missing* that the court is compelled to ascertain the presumed intention of the parties via the 'business efficacy' and the 'officious bystander' tests (both of which are premised on the concept of necessity) ... *although the Belize test is helpful in reminding us of the importance of the general concept of interpretation (and its accompanying emphasis on the need for objective evidence), we would respectfully reject that test in so far as it suggests that the traditional 'business efficacy' and 'officious bystander' tests are not central to the implication of terms. On the contrary, both these tests (premised as they are on the concept of necessity) are an integral as well as indispensable part of the law relating to implied terms in Singapore ....*

The touchstone for implication, in our view, remains that of necessity. The 'business efficacy' and 'officious bystander' tests provide specific guidance for the courts so that the actual process by which terms are implied into a contract will be restrained and purposeful. Indeed the call-and-response nature of these tests has proven to be effective in keeping the courts on a reasonably straight course through water that can be treacherous. The obvious danger with implication, being by its nature an exercise in filling in what parties had not addressed their minds to, is that the court might too easily rewrite the contract to its own preference. Lawyers are not generally noted for an awareness of their own limitations; and there is therefore an inevitable temptation to try to supplement or improve the contract, or to recast it in accordance with the court's sense of the justice of the case, and in the process, losing sight of the actual bargain that was struck between the parties. This is especially dangerous because that bargain would have been struck at a time when parties would have been looking ahead and pricing the inherent uncertainties that this must entail. It is impossible for a court to factor this in meaningfully at the time it comes to examine the issue with the clarity of perfect hindsight. The uncertainty and unpredictability generated by this mismatch are wont to constitute a grave disservice to people of commerce if judges fail to keep such realities firmly in mind.

Indeed this was one of the points made in *The Moorcock*[29] itself, from which the 'business efficacy' test derives. Bowen LJ said that the term implied should be that with 'the minimum of efficacy',[30] and Lord Esher MR thought that it should be the 'least onerous' one possible.[31] Lord Hoffmann too prefaced his exposition in *Belize* with the general observation that the court has no power to improve upon the instrument which it is called upon to construe, and cannot introduce terms to make it fairer or more reasonable.[32] The Singapore courts have taken heed of this, and

[29] *The Moorcock* (1889) 14 PF 64.

[30] ibid 71.

[31] ibid 67.

[32] See n 26, [16]; see also *Panwah Steel Pte Ltd v Koh Brothers Building & Civil Engineering Contractor (Pte) ltd* [2006] 4 SLR(R) 571 [8].

have approached implication conservatively. Where we have differed from Lord Hoffman, however, is his view that the test for the term to be implied should be whether it spells out what the contract, read against the relevant background, would *reasonably* be understood to mean. There is a distinct difference between this and a test which looks to what the contract must *necessarily* be understood to mean. We are inclined to think that replacing necessity with reasonableness as the active ingredient in the implication of terms creates rather too strong a tonic for coping with deficiencies in contractual drafting when these eventually become evident.

There is a third view, however, which is also worth noting. This view proceeds from a different reading of the Privy Council's advice. In the English Court of Appeal's decision in *Mediterranean Salvage*[33] Lord Clarke made the following observation:[34]

> [A]s I read Lord Hoffmann's analysis [in *Belize*], although he is emphasising that the process of implication is part of the process of construction of the contract, he is not in any way resiling from the often stated proposition that it must be necessary to imply the proposed term.
>
> [emphasis added]

A similar view was also expressed by Arden LJ in *Eastleigh BC v Town Quay Developments Ltd*[35] and, outside of the courts, by Lord Grabiner QC.[36] More recently, the Singapore Court of Appeal too has commented that, when read closely, *Belize* may not in fact stand for a stark and dramatic departure from the classical position.

It might also be that, if put into practice, the *Belize* test would not result in much practical difference to the outcome of cases so long as it is *applied* in a stringent fashion. But the stated law should ideally offer clear and principled guidance for prospective cases, and on this basis the Singapore courts have preferred to retain the traditional emphasis on the criterion of necessity and its associated tests.

Revisiting Interpretation and Implication in *Sembcorp*

This brings me to the final and most recent case of the trilogy. In *Sembcorp Marine*[37] the Court of Appeal had the occasion to revisit both *Zurich Insurance* and *Foo Jong Peng*. To take these cases in reverse order, one of

[33] *Mediterranean Salvage and Towage Ltd v Seamar Trading and Commerce Inc; The Reborn* [2010] 1 All ER (Comm) 1.

[34] ibid [15].

[35] *Eastleigh BC v Town Quay Developments Ltd* [2010] 2 P & CR 2 [32].

[36] Lord Grabiner QC, 'The Iterative Process of Contractual Interpretation' (2012) 28 *Law Quarterly Review* 41, 58–61.

[37] *Sembcorp Marine v PPL Holdings* [2013] SGCA 43.

the observations I made in delivering the judgment of the Court was that the gap between *Foo Jong Peng* and *Belize* could be bridged somewhat if one concludes that Lord Hoffmann was saying that the implication of terms is to be seen as part of the overall process of construing the document as a whole.[38] Construction is the composite process that ascertains the parties' actual as well as their presumed intentions from the contract as a whole; it therefore encompasses both the interpretation of express terms and the implication of necessary terms where the express terms have run out.[39] Construction would also include a third process, rectification. Such a reading of Lord Hoffmann's speech in *Belize* also draws support from the judgment of Lord Clarke in *Mediterranean Salvage* which I mentioned earlier. However, there remains a limit to which *Belize* can be reconciled with the law in Singapore. Indeed, in *Sembcorp Marine* we affirmed *Foo Jong Peng* on the standard for the implication of terms being necessity, not reasonableness. It follows that the Singapore courts will also continue to apply the 'business efficacy' and 'officious bystander' tests, although we have further refined their operation.

There has been much debate, both in academic writing and in case law, as to the relationship between these two tests. There are various possible iterations—the two tests can be treated as intrinsically similar or different, conjunctive or disjunctive, and if the latter, they could be inclusively or exclusively so. The Singapore courts have resolved the issue in favour of a 'complementarity' characterisation. This was the conclusion reached by Andrew Phang JA in *Forefront Medical*[40] after an extensive examination of the historical and judicial sources of these tests. It is a position perhaps best exemplified by the following seminal statement of Scrutton LJ in *Reigate*:[41]

> A term can only be implied if it is necessary in the business sense to give efficacy to the contract; that is, if it is such a term that it can confidently be said that if at the time the contract was being negotiated some one had said to the parties, 'What will happen in such a case,' they would both have replied, 'Of course, so and so will happen; we did not trouble to say that; it is too clear.' Unless the Court comes to some such conclusion as that, it ought not to imply a term which the parties themselves have not expressed.

It is clear, from this passage that the officious bystander yardstick serves as an elaboration of the business efficacy test. In *Sembcorp* the Singapore Court of Appeal affirmed and further particularised this characterisation of complementarity. I observed that the application of the business efficacy test serves to aid the court in identifying the lacuna in the contract which

[38] ibid [79].
[39] ibid [31].
[40] *Forefront Medical Technology (Pte) Ltd v Modern-Pak Pte Ltd* [2006] 1 SLR(R) 927.
[41] *Reigate v Union Manufacturing Co (Ramsbottom) Ltd and Elton Copdyeing Co Ltd* [1918] 1 KB 592, 605.

must be filled for it to be commercially workable.[42] Once such a gap has been properly identified, the officious bystander test then enables the court to define that term which can be said to reflect the parties' presumed intentions vis-à-vis that gap.[43] In this way the officious bystander test serves as the practical mode by which the business efficacy test is implemented. I also noted, however, that not all contracts arise in the context of a business transaction; so that there could conceivably be normative standards other than commercial workability which may be preferred in distilling the parties' presumed intentions.

Sembcorp demonstrates that, while preserving the received doctrines of the English common law, we have at the same time made a concerted effort to look behind them to see if their underlying forensic rationales remain alive and well. Where we can, we have introduced interpolations which appear to us to make these doctrines clearer and more systematic for our purposes. This is evident from *Forefront Medical*, *Foo Jong Peng*, and *Sembcorp*. In *Sembcorp*, for instance, we also distilled the law on the implication of contract terms in Singapore to a three-step process—first, to determine how the gap in the contract arose and to confirm that parties had not contemplated the matter or deliberately left that gap uncovered because they were unable to agree on how to address it; second, to ask whether it is necessary in the business or commercial sense to imply a term; and third, to consider the specific term to be implied by applying the officious bystander test.

Turning to contractual interpretation, in *Sembcorp* the Singapore Court of Appeal took another look at the contextual approach to contractual interpretation. We noted that it might well reflect a migration towards the principles adopted in civil law jurisdictions.[44] Such jurisdictions have traditionally taken a permissive approach to the admissibility of extrinsic evidence. Article 1341 of the French Civil Code,[45] for example, allows contracts to be proven by 'any means'. Evidence of pre-contractual negotiations, business practices and customs, and subsequent conduct are all admissible. This, of course, is far more permissive than the position in most if not all common law jurisdictions.

While there is nothing inherently objectionable about a convergence with civil law doctrines, we foresaw serious problems arising at the practical level of implementation if insufficient cognisance was taken of how such civil law principles dovetailed with our legal system. In particular, the liberal admission of extrinsic evidence under the contextual approach to contractual interpretation had to be compatible with the Singapore Evidence

[42] See n 37, [84].
[43] ibid [91].
[44] ibid [34].
[45] Consolidated version of 2 June 2012 read with Art L110-3 of the French Commercial Code.

Act (Cap 97, 1997 Rev Ed) ('the Evidence Act'). Further, any amendments to this area of the law had to take into account the differences between the adversarial litigation process of the common law and the inquisitorial process of civil law systems.

Statutory Differences

The Evidence Act includes provisions that exclude evidence, among them sections 95 and 96. Section 95 excludes evidence for the purpose of explaining or amending a document which on its face is ambiguous or defective. The supplied illustration helps explain this:

> A agrees in writing to sell a horse to B for $500 or $600. Evidence cannot be given to show which price was to be given.

Section 96 excludes evidence given to show that the language of a document, which is plain and accurate in relation to existing facts, was not meant to apply to such facts. In *Sembcorp* we stressed that whilst the Evidence Act was compatible with the contextual approach, any accompanying liberalisation of the extrinsic evidence that is admissible must be limited by these sections of the same Act. To understand the import of these provisions, we undertook a historical examination of the thinking behind the Evidence Act as adapted from the Indian Evidence Act,[46] which had been drafted by Sir James Fitzjames Stephen ('Sir James'). In *Stephen's Digest*,[47] Sir James offered valuable insight into the state of the nineteenth-century English common law which was later meant to be captured in these two sections. We concluded upon an examination of the cases cited there that section 95 operates to exclude extrinsic evidence of the actual intentions of the parties save where there is latent ambiguity in the expression in the instrument.[48] We also concluded that section 96 did not operate to exclude the admission of extrinsic evidence of surrounding circumstances to aid in the interpretation of the instrument. Instead, it reflected the position that parol evidence of the drafter's *subjective* intentions would generally be inadmissible.[49]

Litigation Processes

We also voiced concerns regarding the cost and efficiency of litigation if the civil law rules on the admission of extrinsic evidence were adopted

[46] Evidence Act (Act No 1 of 1872) (India).
[47] Sir Harry Lushington Stephen and Lewis Frederick Sturge (eds), *A Digest of the Law of Evidence*, 12th edn (London, Macmillan and Co Ltd, 1936).
[48] See n 37, [53]–[59].
[49] ibid [63]–[64].

wholesale.[50] There is a legitimate fear that this can lead to parties being inundated by a barrage of documentation which, in an age where everything can be and frequently is digitally stored or recorded, threatens to stymie every step of the litigation process. We heeded the caution sounded by Spigelman CJ[51] against adopting an expansive approach to extrinsic evidence without the 'control valves' which are in place within civil law jurisdictions, including for instance the unavailability of general discovery.[52] Without such controls, a liberal admissibility regime is likely to generate more heat than light, and ultimately drive up both the time taken and the costs expended in litigating a dispute. In commercial terms this would not only be sub-optimal but also inequitable, being to the disadvantage of litigants lacking the financial wherewithal to keep up with the demands of such a liberal regime.

With those concerns in mind, we held in *Sembcorp* that four procedural requirements would be imposed on parties seeking to rely on the contextual approach to support their construction of the contract:[53]

a) They must plead with specificity each fact of the factual matrix which they wish to rely on.
b) It must be pleaded that those factual circumstances were known to all the relevant parties, and how.
c) It must be pleaded what specific effect such facts will have on their contended construction.
d) The obligation of parties to disclose evidence would be limited by the extent to which the evidence would be relevant to the foregoing.

The key point of these requirements is that parties should be clear about the specific aspects and purpose of the factual matrix which they intend to rely on. In other words, the contextual approach set out by the court in *Zurich Insurance* must be implemented with a procedural rigour which prevents the search for the parties' true agreement from descending into an evidential free-for-all.

Interstitial Revisionism

The picture that, I hope, is becoming apparent is that the Singapore courts have begun to re-evaluate various areas of contract law according to our institutional setting and public policy needs. It is an aspect of this process of

[50] ibid [68].

[51] The Honourable James Jacob Spigelman [as he then was], 'Contractual Interpretation: A Comparative Perspective' (2011) 85 *Administrative Law Journal* 412, 431–32.

[52] See also Geoffrey C Hazard Jr, 'Discovery and the Role of the Judge in Civil Law Jurisdictions' (1998) 73 *Notre Dame Law Review* 1017, 1021–2022.

[53] See n 37, [73].

legal contextualisation that we have also cultivated a strong comparativist ethos which looks to the positions of other Commonwealth jurisdictions as well as to the historical sources of the English common law. In *Man Financial v Wong Bark Chuan David*,[54] we were keen to stress that 'in an increasingly interconnected world, local courts ought to eschew legal parochialism and look beyond their shores for relevant precedents—particularly where controversial or … potentially outmoded legal doctrines are concerned.'

We think that this mode of legal development is in keeping with the incrementalism which is inherent in the common law system. At the same time, of course, in seminal cases the common law is capable of taking quantum leaps. Lord Hoffmann's visionary effort at recasting contractual construction as a unitary doctrine of interpretation may yet be regarded by the long arc of legal history as one of those instances. At present, however, and for my part at least, the Singapore courts are more profitably occupied with the interstitial refinement and adaptation of the rules and principles of the common law.

Remoteness of Damage

I turn to the law governing the remoteness of damages in contract. The classical law is of course as stated by Alderson B in *Hadley v Baxendale*,[55] the first limb of which states that the general damages arising from a breach of contract are those which parties would have reasonably contemplated to flow naturally from that breach at the time they made the contract. In other words, only reasonably foreseeable loss is recoverable. Under the second limb, where special circumstances had been communicated between the parties, damages may be awarded based on what parties ought to have contemplated would ordinarily flow from such circumstances.

In *Robertson Quay Investment Pte Ltd v Steen Consultants Pte Ltd*[56] the Singapore Court of Appeal affirmed that *Hadley v Baxendale* continued to represent the law in Singapore as well. Four months after our decision in *Robertson Quay*, however, the House of Lords departed from the rule in *Hadley v Baxendale*, in *The Achilleas*.[57] In an extension of his views on contractual construction, Lord Hoffmann thought that the issue of remoteness of damage was also to be determined according to the objective intentions of the parties. As such, the key question to Lord Hoffmann was whether, on a true construction of the contract, the contract breaker had assumed responsibility for the type of loss in question. In his words, 'the question of

[54] *Man Financial (S) Pte Ltd v Wong Bark Chuan David* [2008] 1 SLR(R) 663 [132].
[55] *Hadley v Baxendale* (1854) 9 Exch 341, 354.
[56] *Robertson Quay Investment Pte Ltd v Steen Consultants Pte Ltd* [2008] 2 SLR(R) 623.
[57] *Transfield Shipping Inc v Mercator Shipping Inc* [2009] 1 AC 61.

whether a given type of loss is one for which a party assumed contractual responsibility involves the interpretation of the contract as a whole against its commercial background, and this, like all questions of interpretation, is a question of law.'[58]

In one of the more expansive statements of his views, Lord Hoffmann also went on to say that 'the implication of a term as a matter of construction of the contract as a whole in its commercial context and the implication of the limits of damages liability seem to me to involve the application of essentially the same techniques of interpretation.'[59]

In the subsequent decision of the Singapore Court of Appeal in *MFM Restaurants*,[60] we declined to follow Lord Hoffmann's lead save to the extent that the concept of assumption of responsibility by the defendant was already incorporated within both limbs of *Hadley v Baxendale*. This view was recently reviewed and restated in *Out of the Box Pte Ltd v Wanin Industries Pte Ltd*.[61] The case concerned the wastage of extensive advertising costs and expenses which the plaintiff had incurred in promoting a sports drink when a shipment supplied by the defendants was found to have changed colour and been contaminated with insects. We dismissed the plaintiff's appeal on the basis that it had the unique business strategy of focusing exclusively on advertising as a means of building a popular brand out of a generic product—as I put it in delivering the judgment of the court, the plaintiff was endeavouring to create a silk purse out of a sow's ears.[62] This exposed the plaintiff to risks which were not made known to the defendant. Indeed, the defendant was wholly ignorant of the plaintiff's unorthodox business strategy—it did not know, for instance, that in relation to a contract which was worth approximately £6,000 in revenue to the defendant, the plaintiff had incurred an inordinate outlay of almost £400,000 in advertising and promotional costs. In such circumstances it was amply clear to us that the plaintiff's losses were too remote to be recoverable.

In reaching this conclusion, we took the opportunity to stress that a clear conceptual distinction must be maintained between the interpretation of a contract to identify the specific nature of the obligation that has been undertaken on the one hand, and the question of the damages for breach of that obligation on the other. We considered that the latter issue must remain one that is to be resolved by reference to the *Hadley v Baxendale* test for remoteness of damage, which looks to the factual matrix in which the parties were situated at the time they entered into the contract. We thought that the conflation proposed by *The Achilleas* would not assist in this exercise,

[58] ibid [25].
[59] ibid [26].
[60] *MFM Restaurants Pte Ltd v Fish & Co Restaurants Pte Ltd* [2011] 1 SLR 150.
[61] *Out of the Box Pte Ltd v Wanin Industries Pte Ltd* [2013] SGCA 15.
[62] ibid [53].

and indeed the perception that damages are a matter of interpretation might well detract from the need to be sensitive to the particular facts of each case.

The concern arises because the assessment of remoteness ought not to be a simplistic and semantic exercise, where heads of liability are first identified and then the actual damages are assessed for fit with those categories. Often, heads of loss which seem to be of a certain type or nature emerge on a proper analysis to be of a quite different type. This is evident from several observations from the bench in *The Achilleas* itself, with both Lord Rodger and Lord Walker noting that while a delay in the redelivery of a vessel might reasonably be expected to result in overruns and a loss of subsequent profitable charters, inordinate losses that were notionally of the same type but caused by volatile economic conditions or loss of contracts that were unusually profitable would be too remote to be recovered.[63] In keeping with these observations, the preferred approach, in our view, is to pay fine-grained attention to the actual loss incurred and to the defendant's knowledge of the facts which led to that loss, and to ask whether a reasonable person in his shoes would have thought at the time of the contract that the loss that materialised was sufficiently foreseeable.

Our study of *The Achilleas* has perhaps revealed a difficulty with pressing unitary juridical devices into multiple modes of service—the danger that we might start to miss the trees for the forest. Interpretation has some bearing on both implication and the remoteness of damages in contract, but if we collapse these devices to a singular unit we begin to gloss over the different considerations which impelled each of them in the first place. Although the law might become easier to grasp and explain, its application will be less structured by second-order rules and principles, and as a result the outcomes of litigation will be more unpredictable. Being able to easily explain the law is insufficient recompense for the difficulties we might expect to encounter with such a unitary theory when tasked with giving *practical advice* to our clients who, by their nature, are generally much more interested in outcomes than in theories.

Duty of Good Faith

Finally, let me take a look at the implication of a duty of good faith into commercial contracts. The key difference between this area of the law of contract and those which we have already examined is that the doctrine of good faith is still a fledgling doctrine, even in English law. In the Singapore Court of Appeal's decision in *Ng Giap Hon v Westcomb Securities Pte Ltd*

[63] See n 56, [60], [82], [83] and [86].

('*Westcomb*'),[64] it was held that a duty to act in good faith could not be implied as a term in law into an agency agreement. Once again, an extensive survey of case law and academic commentary was undertaken and the conclusion drawn was that much about the duty of good faith remained to be settled. The Court's conclusion is representative of the conservatism with which we treat nascent legal doctrines. We said:[65]

> In the circumstances, it is not surprising that the doctrine of good faith continues to be a fledgling one in the Commonwealth. Much clarification is required, even on a theoretical level. Needless to say, until the theoretical foundations as well as the structure of this doctrine are settled, it would be inadvisable (to say the least) to even attempt to apply it in the practical sphere. In the context of the present appeal, this is, in our view, the strongest reason as to why we cannot accede to the appellant's argument that this court should endorse an implied duty of good faith in the Singapore context.
>
> [Internal citations omitted.]

When examining the somewhat more open attitude of the English courts towards the duty of good faith, Andrew Phang JA noted that the receptiveness discernible in cases such as *Interfoto Picture Library Ltd*[66] 'may be due in no small part to the fact that there are, civil law influences that have become relevant as a result of the UK's membership of the European Community.'[67] This is borne out by the following, telling passage from *Cheshire, Fifoot and Furmston's Law of Contract*:[68]

> Do the parties owe each other a duty to negotiate in good faith? Do the parties, once the contract is concluded, owe each other a duty to perform the contract in good faith? Until recently, English lawyers would not have asked themselves these questions or, if asked, would have dismissed them with a cursory 'of course not'. On being told that the German civil code imposed a duty to perform a contract in good faith or that the Italian civil code provides for a duty to negotiate in good faith, a thoughtful English lawyer might have responded by suggesting that the practical problems covered by these code positions were often covered in English law but in different ways. This may still be regarded as the orthodox position but the literature of English law has begun to consider much more carefully whether there might not be merit in explicitly recognising the advantages of imposing good faith duties on negotiation and performance.

Perhaps the clearest exposition of the transmission of good faith from the civil law jurisdictions into English law can be found in the very recent

[64] *Ng Giap Hon v Westcomb Securities Pte Ltd* [2009] 3 SLR(R) 518.

[65] ibid [32].

[66] *Interfoto Picture Library Ltd v Stiletto Visual Programmes Ltd* [1989] QB 433.

[67] See n 64, [53]

[68] MP Furmston, *Cheshire, Fifoot and Furmston's Law of Contract*, 15th edn (Oxford, Oxford University Press, 2007) 32–33.

English High Court decision of *Yam Seng Pte Ltd v International Trade Corporation Ltd*.[69] The learned judge offered the following account:[70]

> In refusing, however, if indeed it does refuse, to recognise any such general obligation of good faith, this jurisdiction would appear to be swimming against the tide. As noted by Bingham LJ in the *Interfoto* case, a general principle of good faith (derived from Roman law) is recognised by most civil law systems—including those of Germany, France and Italy. From that source references to good faith have already entered into English law via EU legislation. For example, the Unfair Terms in Consumer Contracts Regulations 1999, which give effect to a European directive, contain a requirement of good faith. Several other examples of legislation implementing EU directives which use this concept are mentioned in *Chitty on Contracts*, 31st Ed, volume 1 at para 1-043. Attempts to harmonise the contract law of EU member states, such as the Principles of European Contract Law proposed by the Lando Commission and the European Commission's proposed Regulation for a Common European Sales Law on which consultation is currently taking place, also embody a general duty to act in accordance with good faith and fair dealing. There can be little doubt that the penetration of this principle into English law and the pressures towards a more unified European law of contract in which the principle plays a significant role will continue to increase.

The same pressures are, needless to say, not applicable in Singapore. We are therefore more likely to fall back on the implication of terms in fact to look for a duty of good faith, even as the English courts seem poised to take up a more absolute position. This much was acknowledged by the Court of Appeal in *Westcomb*.[71] On the other hand, it is the position in Singapore law that the courts are likely to give effect to an express term to negotiate in good faith. In *Toshin Development*,[72] the Singapore Court of Appeal held that an express term to negotiate the market rental value of specified premises in good faith was enforceable. VK Rajah JA, in delivering the judgment of the Court, observed that such clauses are in the public interest, as they promote the consensual disposition of potential disputes. Rajah JA also noted that good faith clauses are consistent with our cultural values of promoting consensus wherever possible.[73] While this pacifist streak of Singapore society is not always on display in our courts, it is nevertheless interesting to note that there are social drivers which may eventually propel our jurisprudence in the same direction as England's.

Perhaps the best summary of the status of good faith in Singapore contract law is that we have not foreclosed its recognition as a general duty, even if we remain sceptical that such a development will materialise in the

[69] *Yam Seng Pte Ltd v International Trade Corporation Ltd* [2013] 1 Lloyd's Rep 526.
[70] ibid [124].
[71] See n 64, [61].
[72] *HSBC Institutional Trust Services (Singapore) Ltd (trustee of Starhill Global Real Estate Investment Trust) v Toshin Development Singapore Pte Ltd)* [2012] 4 SLR 738.
[73] ibid [40].

near future. Our courts have continued to track the progress of the doctrine throughout the Commonwealth, although we are careful to note that it cannot migrate into our legal system without first undergoing a process of naturalisation.

Evaluating the Difference

As I approach the close of my lecture I would like to make good on my initial promise to evaluate whether the divergences which I have identified constitute a problem in search of a solution. There is, to begin with, a matter of perception to be considered. Some might find it peculiar that Singapore appears to have become a repository, and even a conservatory, of classical English law, whilst the English courts have become increasingly eclectic and perhaps even iconoclastic. This would of course be a misrepresentation—the common law has never been a static institution.[74]

As should be clear from my examination of the cases, the overriding narrative of Singapore law has been that of fidelity to the pillars of the English common law, without being hidebound by its dogma. We have adapted the law to our own circumstances, just as English jurisprudence has adapted to a more Eurocentric political and economic reality. We have also tried to clarify and, at least as we see it, to improve upon English authorities, just as the English courts have always sought to bring greater internal coherence to English case law. In so doing, I would say that both jurisdictions are exemplifying the common law's ability to absorb and accommodate change. In an ever-shrinking world, we must recognise and indeed expect that the great canvas of the common law will be filled with the contributions of judges from all over the world. Yet it is as if we each take a screenshot of that canvas and then go away and work on it in our own studios, so that the resulting works might sometimes look quite different yet also quite familiar. Looking at the works of others might well cause us to rethink, if not revisit, the products of our own efforts.

This raises the question of the impact of legal divergences on economic integration. The grand project of the harmonisation of law has as many ardent defenders as passionate detractors,[75] and it is beyond the ambition

[74] Indeed the influence of continental jurisprudence upon English contract law is nothing new, as can be gleaned from Michael Furmston, *Cheshire, Fifoot & Furmston's Law of Contract*, 16th edn (Oxford, Oxford University Press, 2012) 22.

[75] For a useful overview, see Martin Shapiro, 'The Globalization of Law' (1993–1994) 1 *Indiana Journal of Global Legal Studies* 37; see also Martin Boodman 'The Myth of Harmonization of Laws' (1991) 39 *American Journal of Comparitive Law* 699; Ralf Michaels and Nils Jansen, 'Private Law Beyond the State? Europeanization, Globalization, Privatization' (2006) 54 *American Journal of Comparitive Law* 843; and R Goode, 'Contract and Commercial Law: the Logic and Limits of Harmonisation' (2003) *Ius Commune* Lecture.

of this lecture to land a decisive blow for either corner. What is empirically verifiable is that the existence of different legal systems increases the transaction costs of cross-border business. Not only do investors have to expend resources on securing compliance with national regulations, they will also have to price in the additional risks which accompany the enforcement of cross-border contracts when disputes arise. It has been suggested that the uncertainty which exists between the boundaries of different legal systems lowers investment, consumption and overall economic performance.[76] To the extent that the costs of implementing common commercial laws are outweighed by the benefits of reductions in transactional and regulatory barriers to entry, it cannot be gainsaid that harmonisation is a positive force. I wish, however, to make two observations.

The first is that, even as transnational trade has become an economic imperative, there remains room for considered difference in fundamental areas of commercial law. Such differences do not pose major problems so long as parties are well-advised and the law as a whole does not slide into parochialism. The doctrine of private international law performs an essential mediating function when disputes arise between commercial parties from different jurisdictions, and in this way a *modus vivendi* has been established so that the wheels of commerce do not stop turning when legal complications arise. The availability of international commercial arbitration has also removed some of the pressure created by the diversity of commercial laws, as parties are able to privately agree among themselves on a process run on a more or less common set of rules to govern the way they settle their differences, if not quite yet to regulate the substance of their transactions. We should not forget that outside of mandatory rules and terms implied in law, contracts remain modes of private law-ordering which allow parties to set their terms, and that commercial parties—with the assistance of their lawyers—are adaptable creatures.

The second is that some differences are justified when they are the result of domestic imperatives, considered government policy or structural differences across jurisdictions. As much as the harmonisation of commercial law will represent an economic boon, nation states are more than mere trading entities and may justifiably prioritise other areas of public policy over economic liberalism. Indeed, even where harmonisation is a dominant concern, it should be approached with sensitivity towards ensuring its practical implementation. Otherwise, the result of superficial harmony will be a persistent substantive disparity in outcomes. A point I raised earlier in the context of contractual interpretation illustrates this. In *Sembcorp* we were concerned that the unqualified combination of liberal civil law doctrines

[76] Helmut Wagner, 'Costs of Legal Uncertainty: is Harmonization of Law a Good Solution?' delivered at the fortieth annual session of UNCITRAL (available online: www.uncitral.org/pdf/english/congress/WagnerH.pdf) p 1.

on the admissibility of extrinsic evidence with the common law pre-trial discovery process might result in an overwhelming amount of material being dredged up every time a matter comes to trial. We therefore concluded that the drift towards the civilian approach of contractual interpretation had to be accompanied by adjustments following a careful analysis of how this drift will be actualised in practice. In short, harmonisation will have to be piloted in a controlled fashion.

Looking Ahead

Subject to these observations, I remain bullish on the prospects of harmonisation, going forward. Leaving aside the creation of common doctrines of commercial law, there are manifest opportunities for harmonisation on other levels. The international arbitration experience offers a loose narrative by which such harmonisation can be scripted—at least for its first two Acts.

The Opening Act could be the harmonisation of recognition and enforcement, which makes the most direct practical impact for the end-users of commercial litigation. In arbitration, this was achieved by successive international instruments, beginning in 1923 with the Geneva Protocol on Arbitration Clauses, followed by the 1927 Geneva Convention, the 1958 New York Convention, and in 1985 the UNCITRAL Model Law. The Hague Convention on Choice of Court Agreements has the potential to do the same for foreign judgments in civil and commercial matters. Under the Hague Convention, parties may choose to resolve their dispute in the court of a state party whereupon proceedings in other member states will be suspended or dismissed.[77] The chosen court cannot decline to hear the case on the grounds of *forum non conveniens*,[78] and the judgment of that court will be recognised and enforced in any other member state of the Convention.[79] Two of the world's largest economies, the US and EU, have already signed the Convention, which will come into effect with the ratification of just one more state. I am cautiously optimistic that if and when this happens, it will represent a watershed for the international recognition and enforcement of foreign judgments.[80]

At the same time, we should expect that the application of the Hague Convention will be subject to some heterogeneity. Complete uniformity of outcomes in the enforcement of foreign judgments is a chimera, and indeed

[77] Convention on Choice of Court Agreements (concluded 30 June 2005) Art 6.

[78] ibid, Art 5.

[79] Convention on the Recognition and Enforcement of Foreign Judgments in Civil and Commercial Matters (concluded 1 February 1971), Ch 2.

[80] On a bilateral level, harmonisation can also be achieved by entering into a Memorandum of Guidance which sets out a clear understanding of the enforcement procedures for money judgments in each other's courts—see below.

one of the concerns that is sometimes raised is that the Hague Convention has not left a sufficient margin of appreciation for member states to take account of domestic policy imperatives.[81] Nevertheless, it must be conceded that the extent of divergence will be far less than it stands at present. Too much uncertainty attends the current regime, where the enforceability of foreign judgments turns entirely on the private international law of the enforcing state. The cost of such uncertainty simply fails to add up for sophisticated commercial parties. While the Hague Convention might not result consistently in the mutual enforcement of judgments within its member states, the hope is that it will nonetheless be a positive step towards promoting the use of litigation as a viable alternative means of transnational dispute resolution to international commercial arbitration.

Here, let me digress with a brief interlude into the role of national courts in relation to the recognition and enforcement of international arbitration awards. This is useful, if only to make the point that even under the New York Convention and the Model Law, there can be undulations in the way those instruments are actually applied by enforcing courts, notwithstanding the fact that there are 149 contracting states to the New York Convention[82] and 67 states that have enacted a version of the UNCITRAL Model Law.[83]

In a recent decision, *PT First Media TBK v Astro Nusantara International BV and others* ('*Astro*'),[84] the Singapore Court of Appeal had occasion to survey the international arbitration regime set up by these instruments. The key threshold issue before the Court was whether the appellant was within its rights to try to resist the enforcement of an arbitration award on the ground that the tribunal lacked jurisdiction, having previously opted not to take any of the available avenues to actively challenge the same tribunal's preliminary finding that it had jurisdiction. Our attention was therefore focused on the scope and content of a national court's discretion to refuse the recognition and enforcement of an international arbitration award. We found that the Model Law, like the New York Convention, was designed to de-emphasise the importance of the seat of arbitration and to facilitate the uniform treatment of awards, regardless of where they were sited. This, of course, is in line with the observations of the UK Supreme Court in *Dallah*.[85] Equally, and subject to the operation of waiver and issue estoppel, we held that arbitrating parties would not be precluded from resisting the enforcement of an

[81] See Mary Keyes, 'Jurisdiction under the Hague Choice of Courts Convention; Its Likely Impact on Australian Practice' (2009) 5 *Journal of Private International Law* 181.

[82] www.uncitral.org/uncitral/en/uncitral_texts/arbitration/NYConvention_status.html.

[83] www.uncitral.org/uncitral/en/uncitral_texts/arbitration/1985Model_arbitration_status.html.

[84] *PT First Media TBK v Astro Nusantara International BV and others* [2013] SGCA 57.

[85] *Dallah Real Estate and Tourism Holding Co v Ministry of Religious Affairs of the Government of Pakistan* [2010] UKSC 46 [28] (Lord Mance).

award even when they had previously eschewed the opportunity to raise an appeal or set it aside. In other words, parties have what can be aptly termed a 'choice of remedies'.

The necessary price of this system is that inconsistencies can arise at the stage of enforcement. In *Dallah* itself we saw that the English Supreme Court refused to enforce a French award on the ground that there was insufficient evidence that Pakistan had intended to be bound by the arbitration agreement. The French Court of Appeal disagreed. It held that Pakistan's conduct during the negotiation process clearly demonstrated that it was a party to the transaction and therefore subject to the arbitration agreement.

The reality is that the present international arbitration regime allows different enforcement outcomes to be reached within an otherwise uniform approach to the enforceability of awards. Indeed, this is part of the design of the international commercial arbitration regime. The harmonisation which is envisaged by the New York Convention and, by extension, the Model Law is that any of the contracting states can determine for itself whether any particular arbitral award should be recognised and enforced, but within a common framework, setting out a common set of grounds. The fact that the passive remedy of resisting recognition and enforcement can be dispensed by any contracting state where enforcement is sought means that national courts can and must be fully engaged at this stage. They perform the vital function of quality control for arbitration. If the decisions of arbitrators are enforced unquestioningly, we run the risk of undermining the integrity of the system of international arbitration, which relies on the national courts to act as the final arbiters on the legal fitness of awards.

Given this scheme of the New York Convention and the Model Law, it is ultimately not helpful to speak in terms of whether a jurisdiction is pro- or anti- arbitration, depending on how frequently or easily arbitral awards are enforced there. Such characterisations do not account for whether or not curial intervention on the grounds set out in the New York Convention or the Model Law is in fact justified in the circumstances. It is much more useful to look at the reasoning adopted by different courts. On a more general level it is also important that national courts are aware of how their counterparts are carrying out their function as the gatekeepers of the system.

Let me return to the main discussion. If Act One concerns the harmonisation of the rules of enforcement, Act Two would be the harmonisation of the dispute resolution process. I do not mean to suggest that we disturb the way that litigation is conducted in national courts. Rather, I think that streamlined procedures for the resolution of international commercial disputes can be developed alongside and parallel to the normal litigation process. The most practical way to do this would be through the creation of commercial courts with specialised rules of procedure which can be harmonised on a regional or even international level. The creation of a custom-built annex for commercial disputes can be achieved without remodelling the existing architecture of national court systems. Commercial parties will then have recourse to a fully constituted court, with all its attendant coercive facilities, which is also sensitive to the needs and realities of international business. De facto models of such courts already exist, in the form of the London Commercial Court, the Delaware Court of Chancery and the Commercial Court of the Supreme Court of Victoria, to name just a few. International courts have also been set up in the Dubai International Financial Centre and in Qatar. Singapore is presently developing a framework for the establishment of the Singapore International Commercial Court ('the SICC'), with a Bench that will likely comprise some of our existing Supreme Court judges, as well as eminent Singaporean and international commercial law jurists.

The premise of the SICC is that, as Asia's economic growth continues, cross-border disputes will inevitably increase and demand will grow for a court-based dispute resolution mechanism to deal with cases which are not amenable to arbitration or might be better suited for a variety of reasons to litigation. We believe that Singapore can leverage upon its commercial position and the international standing of its judiciary to meet this demand. We expect that the court will hear three categories of cases. The first is where parties have consented to use the SICC *after* their dispute has arisen. The second is where parties have agreed in a prior contract that the SICC will have jurisdiction over any disputes which arise between them. The third category will be cases within the jurisdiction of the Singapore High Court which are transferred to the SICC at the discretion of the Chief Justice. The precise mechanics of this Court are still in the early stages of development, and I look forward to making available a more detailed prospectus of the SICC soon.

As part of Act Two, I believe there is value to be had in developing deeper connections among these commercial courts and exploring further avenues not just for knowledge-sharing but also substantive collaboration. The first steps have already been taken. The Supreme Court of Singapore entered into a Memorandum of Understanding ('MOU') with the Supreme Court of New South Wales in 2010, under which we may refer questions of New South Wales law to the New South Wales Supreme Court, and vice-versa. This has been acknowledged as an innovative procedure and our New South Wales counterparts have since signed a similar MOU with the New York state courts. I mention these instruments as examples of how inter-curial collaboration can assure commercial parties of the correct application of foreign law regardless of the jurisdiction in which they choose to resolve their dispute. In the same vein, a Memorandum of Guidance was signed by the Dubai International Financial Centre courts and the London Commercial Court earlier this year which sets out the procedures for the enforcement of money judgments in the respective institutions. The introduction to this Memorandum of Guidance states that while its terms are not legally binding, the main object is to promote a mutual comprehension of both parties' laws and judicial processes and to improve public perception and understanding.[86] This is a useful reminder that, apart from the confidence that inter-curial collaboration can engender, the sharing and circulation of information about the workings of other courts will also be of intrinsic value as litigation becomes increasingly international in nature.

In keeping with this, for some time now, the commercial judges of Sydney, Hong Kong and Singapore, three of the leading commercial and financial centres in Asia have been meeting every other year to discuss cutting-edge issues in commercial litigation. We hosted the conference this year and were joined for the first time by the judges from the High Court of Mumbai as well as commercial judges from a number of other Asian jurisdictions and we hope by the next round to have commercial judges from Shanghai join us.

To my mind, strengthening the community of commercial courts might even present the surest route towards Act Three—a deeper harmonisation of substantive law. As these courts specialise in deciding international commercial disputes, they are particularly well situated to develop a consistent jurisprudence of international commercial law. We might even envision a future where such a coherent corpus of case law has been propagated by commercial courts that it could be looked upon as a source of *lex mercatoria*. An international community of commercial courts will represent a practical solution to multinational businesses which require a reliable, neutral, and legitimised mechanism for dispute resolution, and in so doing transform the anxiety over uncommon laws of commerce into an opportunity for further integration between law and commerce. The law has always been part of the infrastructure for international trade, but with some forward thinking by lawyers and legal institutions, it might aim to become part of the modern *superstructure* as well.

Conclusion

If any part of this script is to be translated into reality, then we must begin with a dialogue among stakeholders in the regional and international spheres. Singapore has already been involved in discussions on further legal cooperation and harmonisation within ASEAN. The Centre for International Law ('CIL') at the National University of Singapore has been a leader in this initiative. The ASEAN Integration Through Law project which I mentioned earlier has been one of its major research activities. It presently involves 77 investigators working on about 40 studies on ASEAN legal

[86] Memorandum of Guidance as to Enforcement between the DIFC Courts and the Commercial Court, Queen's Bench Division, England and Wales (available online: www.judiciary.gov.uk/Resources/JCO/Documents/Guidance/uk-uae-protocol-with-logos.pdf) paras 2 and 3.

integration.[87] Among the key deliverables of this multilateral discourse will be a rich toolkit of models, options, methods and analyses which would then be at the disposal of policy makers, practitioners and academics.

We are also looking beyond the immediate region, to a wider sphere. In my keynote address at the 26th LAWASIA Conference last month, I suggested the commissioning of an international conference to discuss the prospects of the harmonisation of commercial law among countries in Asia and the Pacific. Apart from galvanising what has hitherto been a decentralised discourse, such a conference would also yield tangible deliverables for a range of stakeholders including commercial judges, lawyers, academics and in-house counsel. For the representatives of states from outside of the Asia-Pacific region, it will operate as a one-stop showcase of the nature and development of Asia-Pacific law. For MNCs and other commercial interests, the conference will be an opportunity to actively participate in foundational discussions about the prospects of developing a legal infrastructure which will be of direct benefit to their businesses. Finally, international organisations such as the Hague Conference, UNIDROIT and UNCITRAL might take the conference as an opportunity to form meaningful partnerships to further augment their work. I also announced last week that the Singapore Academy of Law will convene the first of what I hope will be a regular series of such conferences, within the next 18 months.

We have already seen the source of the influences which propel our jurisprudence in new directions. For England, the traditions of European civil law will continue to exert a gravitational force. As the orbit of English law shifts, it will inevitably have a bearing on other jurisdictions, including Singapore. Thus far, our approach can perhaps be best described as adoption with adaptation. Indeed, we hope that the work of our courts will also percolate back into the groundwater of the common law perhaps causing some refinements here such that through this process of exchange, we might yet find a common meeting ground. This describes the way the common law has developed historically, save that judges from more parts of the world now have an increasingly important contribution to make. The vision of harmonisation is wider than what we common lawyers have perhaps always taken for granted. The next frontier has already been scouted, and the great challenge ahead of us must be the recruitment of jurisdictions like China, Indochina, Indonesia, the Middle East and continental Europe to participate in a global conversation on a commercial law framework that strives to serve the transnational trading environment of this twenty-first century.

[87] See: http://cil.nus.edu.sg/research-projects/cil-research-projects/asean/overview/.

9

Advocacy—What Works and What Doesn't

LORD JUSTICE VOS

Lord Justice Vos gave this lecture in October 2014 as part of COMBAR's series of Professional Education of Lectures at the Royal College of Surgeons.

I AM VERY grateful to Sonia Tolaney QC for inviting me to give this address. It was suggested that my subject should be 'appellate advocacy'. Since I have only been listening to appellate advocacy in a professional capacity for 12 months, I might not have been the right person to ask in the first place. I shall try to avoid causing offence, but then you cannot make an omelette without breaking the odd egg.

I have long pondered the question of what difference advocacy makes to the outcome of litigation. The answer is, I think, 'it depends'. I shall come to this after a few words about advocacy in the Court of Appeal and about cross-examination.

Court of Appeal Advocacy

You may think the Court of Appeal is irritable and impatient, and does not listen to what you say. That is not true, but you may think it is because advocacy has to be tailored to the audience. If you are making a jury speech for the benefit of your client or your solicitors—to demonstrate that you have done everything possible to win the case, then you are bound to irritate the Court of Appeal.

The Court of Appeal these days actually does do a great deal of pre-reading. But that does not mean that the outcome of a case is pre-determined before you get to court. Cases can be turned round: even more than once—with one judge, or with three, or even five. But to do that, you need to work out—or listen out—carefully. You need to address your submissions to the problem as the court sees it. Or, alternatively, if there is no problem from the court's point of view, to explain concisely at the outset what is the primary problem that you say exists with the judgment below. In short, you need to get your screwdriver into the judgment quickly. If you fail to do that, you may be on a losing wicket.

Let me try to unpack that summary of what advocacy needs to be all about in the Court of Appeal.

You will have put in a detailed skeleton argument before you start, and you can be confident that it has been read. By the way, it is worth noting that excessively lengthy skeletons in the Court of Appeal are very much to be deprecated. We never have sufficient time to read them except when the estimate for the case is exceptionally long, which it almost never is nowadays. You really can say all you need in any appeal in 25 pages of 12 point type. For goodness sake, don't use smaller, natty, pretty fonts—some of us have bad eyes and will not be able to read it, with the best will in the world.

I have never known a Court of Appeal that took more than 20 minutes to say something, once the argument began. Normally 20 seconds is a better estimate. This is your chance to divine what is going on within the court. The kind of thing that is said depends on the Presider. It may be coded; it may be direct; it may be positive; and it may be negative. But whatever it is, it is crucial. It is almost certainly something the court has discussed before it came in and wants to get off its chest. Like—we would be particularly interested to hear argument on such and such a point. That generally means that this is your best or worst point. Either way, follow the lead, and don't say: I have 43 points and I will get to that one just after lunch.

The key to success in the Court of Appeal is flexibility. You may have detailed notes of what you think you are going to say. Only rarely will you be able or will it be sensible for you to say what you have noted down. It is always going to be better to tackle head-on what is worrying the court.

Where then do you start? Because the start is important: the most important thing to start with is where the judge went wrong. If possible, this should be short, crisp and compelling. It is the screwdriver bit. All Courts of Appeal take the judge's decision seriously, but once they are satisfied that a material error was made, they can start to help you dismantle the judgment.

How then do you handle the wingmen or wingwomen on the court? Well, I would say this; but they are normally just as important as the man or woman in the middle. The point is that one of the three has been pre-nominated to write the lead judgment. You need to work out who that is. Sometimes it is easy: if there is one commercial and two family judges, and you are doing a commercial case, it will not be hard. But often, it is not quite so easy. The nominated judge will sometimes say less than the others, since he or she will often have read more. The reason why you want to look after each member of the court, starting of course with the one you perceive to be the most influential, is because they all matter. Sometimes, the nominated judge calls all the shots, but not as often as you think; all members of the court are generally engaged and will have things that they will try to persuade the nominated judge about. Of course, sometimes that results in more than one judgment, but not all that often. More often, the discussion behind the scenes feeds into and influences the lead judgment, with which the others agree.

A word then about the use of authorities. I think this is an area where advocates make the most mistakes. It follows on from what I have been saying about wing-judges. The court's underlying knowledge of the authorities in a particular area is likely to be highly variable. Even if judges speak about '*The Fanti*', or '*The Olympic Pride*', or whatever case, with apparent total recall, they almost certainly will *not* have total recall of what it actually says. The rest of the court may never have heard of it. So, it is no use bandying names of cases about like sugar puffs, without explaining what the cases are supposed to say.

Courts are always reluctant actually to look at authorities. But sometimes they need to be forced to do so. If you are going to a case, it is crucial to tell the court first the proposition which the authority is meant to elucidate. The Presider may then say that there is no need to look at it for that proposition. So be ready to explain why there is a need, if you really think there is.

Be sparing with authority for general propositions—and just give references. Only go to authorities that are truly in point in relation to the precise issue under appeal. Then take enough time with those crucial cases to ensure that each member of the court understands the facts, the case, and the point you are getting out of it.

Try to avoid a huge chronological trawl through all the authorities on the point unless you are genuinely trying, and likely to be able, to get the court to make new law.

My bête noire is huge bundles of authorities that are never looked at. And the provision of six 'agreed' bundles of authorities, none of which is looked at, when the only case that matters is one that is handed up at the last minute in the course of submissions. This happens literally all the time. The time spent in putting together, with your opponent, a sensible slim bundle of relevant authorities that will be referred to or is at least relevant to what needs to be decided, is time very well spent.

And please tell your solicitors to number bundles in big letters, or numbers in three places—it is so silly to have every bundle with masses of tiny print including every party, every judge, every number, but with the bundle number in two point only on the spine.

Next and equally important is the provision of statutes and textbooks. The most annoying habit is to produce isolated sections of the crucial legislation in the case, so that the context cannot be understood. Of course, we can and do get everything on the internet, but the whole of the relevant parts of the statute that underlies the case needs to be produced without bits excised! Likewise textbooks. If they are worth putting in the bundle (which they are often not), then it is worth including the whole or at least the bulk of the chapter on the relevant topic.

I should say something about timing. Timing is crucial. Many advocates think we are obsessed about it. I am afraid we need to be. We simply cannot go over the estimate even if we want to. Tell the court right at the beginning what you have agreed with your opponent about how long each of you will be and when the case will finish. Also set out how you intend to deal with your submissions, even if it doesn't work out like that because you are diverted by the points that interest the court.

By the way, court interruptions are generally good for you, but they do not entitle you to go over time, save in the most exceptional of circumstances, so don't start to wax lyrical just because the court appears to be on your side—if you need to move on, make sure you do so, to cover other points properly before the time runs out.

The next thing is dealing with irritability. Nowadays very few judges are really irritable—even if they were in the good old days. We are pussycats by comparison. If you really get on the wrong side of a judge, you will sometimes find one of the others comes to the rescue. But the watchword in such a situation is to be brief, to the point and play the thing with a straight bat.

Now what about jokes? I used to love making jokes in court. And most of the time I got away with it. If you are three years' call in the Court of Appeal, I suggest you leave the jokes out. That said, humour is a great aide to advocacy, so at an appropriate time, a light touch can help.

Finally, on this point, a word about replies. Cases can be and often are won in reply. The biggest mistake advocates make is not to realise that. You may well see the court swing over against you when the respondent's counsel has been going a little while. By then you will have a much clearer idea of where the court stands.

To prepare a proper reply, you have to listen carefully to the other side—however irritating that process can be. One famous leading advocate of my generation used to walk out of court when his opponent was speaking, as he said he couldn't stand listening to all that garbage. But, unfortunately, it is only by listening attentively to the other advocate that you can hope to work out where the holes are in his or her argument. You should then mercilessly expose those logical fallacies or non sequiturs in your reply.

So it is absolutely crucial not to waste your reply. It must be short, and punchy. Make enumerated points that you have written down to address head-on the points your opponent has made. Don't assume the court has got the answers to these points to hand from your opening. It is your last and most important opportunity to get the appeal decided in your favour.

I cannot believe the number of advocates who say in reply: 'Oh well, you know all the points I would make from my opening, so I will only deal with the case of *Snooks*', which is always the one that was quite irrelevant to the substance of the appeal. Use your reply. Make it succinct and totally focused.

The Court of Appeal does try very hard to get the right answer. If you think your case deserves a longer hearing, write in to explain why. Sometimes you will be right, and that will be accepted by the Presider. Well, so much for the Court of Appeal.

Cross-Examination

I told Sonia that I would say something about cross-examination, and I will, but only in the most general terms. I have not seen very many brilliant cross-examinations. It is very difficult to do. You know the basic rules:

1. Don't ask open-ended questions, only closed questions that are answered with a yes or a no.
2. Don't ask composite or lengthy questions that are hard to understand.
3. Don't ask that final question which will kill your case.
4. On each topic or each document, know precisely in advance why you are asking about it and where you are hoping to end up.
5. Don't bully witnesses. The court will then have sympathy for them, however crooked you may think they are.
6. Don't go through documents just for the sake of it, unless you have something specific to ask.
7. Establish the uncontentious parameters first. You will want to use these later when, as you will know in advance, the witness is going to have to contradict some of them in order to maintain his case.

This is all pretty basic, and far easier to say than to do. I think, once again, that timing is everything. A long-winded boring pointless cross-examination is worse than not bothering to do it. Obviously you must put your case, but that can be done quickly and succinctly.

The key actually is to have a plan—here, notes do pay off, even if you don't follow them precisely.

Bear in mind that the truth is often not as black and white as your client may have told you. It is generally a very bland shade of grey. And also bear in mind that almost all witnesses believe they are telling the truth, even if they are not. This is for a variety of reasons, including:

1. The fact that they have persuaded themselves they are right, whatever actually happened—now rather a long time ago.
2. They are generally not particularly clever, so don't really remember what happened, and it suits them to tell this particular story.
3. The rarest option. They are actually essentially dishonest, and truth means nothing to them—or at least not as much as money means to them.
4. But even more importantly, try to find and identify the grey middle area, because that is often good enough for your case. The black or white conclusion is not always the only way of winning.
5. Finally, try to get the witness to like you. It doesn't always work, because the other side will have painted you as an ogre. But it never hurts to be nice through as much of the cross-examination as possible—even when you are calling the witness a bare-faced liar.

Does it Make a Difference?

So let me come back to the question I started with: does advocacy make a difference? Can you change the result of a case just by being a good barrister?

Well this, as I say, is a tricky question.

I would start by answering it like this: every piece of commercial or chancery litigation, particularly a heavy one-but not only a heavy one—is like a game of chess. There are many moves. You cannot make every move correctly, but you can hope to make more correct moves than your opponents. I knew people at the Bar who had the knack of taking wrong turnings in cases. They generally did not do very well. The point is that to succeed in litigation, you need to make more of the right moves than your opponent over time.

The other key thing is to review your case strategy as frequently as possible, to make sure it is still taking full and proper account of the huge number of changes of circumstance that occur in every piece of litigation. Some strategies will be decided by your solicitors or clients, but you should try to influence them—most important of all is to gain the confidence of the clients so they will take your strategic advice rather than, as is quite common, completely ignore it—and still expect you to win the case.

But I have digressed slightly. Can what you do make a difference? Well if your client is an out-and-out liar and cross-examination demonstrates that, the answer is almost certainly not. But assuming that is not the case, and the case is finely balanced, advocacy can, I think, make a difference-but only sometimes.

It is not always good, though, to be too successful—because if you win a legal point you should not have won, you will set up an appeal that you are likely to lose. Even if the advocacy does not win a bad case, it ensures that you do not lose a good one, and that the court does not hare off too often on a frolic of its own, which can and does happen—even sometimes in the Court of Appeal.

Conclusions

Remember in all your professional activities in court that judges are human. The merits are important, and if they look as if they are against you, you need to spend some time—preferably very subtly, even gently—explaining why your victory would not be the disaster that the judges might at first sight think.

Finally, I would repeat just one point: be flexible. That is crucial. It requires hard work in preparation. But it is worth it. You often have to throw away what you have prepared, but provided you have done your homework, you will be fine.

10

A Brief Account of the Origins and Development of the Commercial Court and the Challenges it Faces at this Point in its History

SIR RICHARD FIELD

Sir Richard Field was the guest Judge at the 2014 North American meeting that was held in Seville, Spain, at the Alfonso XIII Hotel. His lunchtime talk was given in the glorious sunshine in the gardens of the hotel.

Sir Richard Field retired from the High Court with effect from 1 September 2014.

IN THIS SHORT address I propose to give a brief account of the origins and development of the Commercial Court and the challenges it faces at this point in its history. I am also going to tell you about the other life of the Commercial Court judge when he goes back into the Queen's Bench Division and departs on circuit to try class A crime, mostly murders. I shall illustrate this latter part of my talk by relating one or two events, all of which I have been assured are true.

There is one man above all others to thank for the creation of the Commercial Court.

Mr Justice Lawrance was appointed to the High Court by the then Lord Chancellor, Lord Halsbury, who was renowned for putting allegiance to the Tory Party above legal competence when it came to appointing High Court judges. Lawrance was a Tory. Most informed opinion holds that Lawrance was barely up to the Victorian County Court Bench, if that.

In May 1890, Lawrance J was the trial judge in *Rose v Bank Australasia*. The claim was for general average. A sailing ship carrying Australian wool had been wrecked on the rocks at Cape Gris-Nez. A quantity of the cargo was saved; the rest was lost or stolen by local French residents, grateful to the Almighty for so generously answering their prayers. The issue for trial was how the cost of the lost cargo was to be ratably shared amongst all the cargo owners. The cream of the Commercial Bar were instructed. Arthur Cohen QC leading TE Scrutton, the latter just a year from taking silk, appeared for the claimant, the vessel's owners. Gorrell Barnes QC and Joseph Walton appeared for the defendant consignees.

The case lasted two weeks. The documents were many and stacked high. Lawrance J took a full note but understood barely a word. He reserved his judgment. After six months, counsel politely enquired when his decision could be expected, and the case was eventually listed for judgment. What happened was described many years later by Lord Justice Scrutton. The judge came into court and said: 'This is an interesting case raising questions of general average. The first question is: what was the first question Mr Cohen?' Mr Cohen told him what the first question was. The judge continued: 'Yes, I agree with the average-stater. And the second question: the second question, Mr Barnes, what exactly was it?' And so with the third question: 'I agree with the average-stater; judgment for the plaintiff.'

In January 1892 a joint report of the Bar Committee and the Law Society concluded: 'if the High Court of Justice is to regain the confidence of the commercial community, or even retain its present limited share in the settlement of mercantile disputes, it is imperative that a separate commercial list should be established.'

Finally, on 1 February 1895, the Commercial Court opened for business under the experienced eye of Mr Justice Matthew.

The current judges in the Commercial Court stand on the shoulders of their predecessors. Men like Scrutton, Atkin, McNair, Denning, Devlin, Diplock, Kerr and Mustill ensured the success of the Court. In October 2011, the Court moved to a brand new building—the Rolls Building—equipped for the modern age. It is now busier than ever, taking its place at the centre of London's legal services market whose value to the UK economy is £20.4 billion, representing 1.5% of GDP.

The Court's range of work is broad. In the last couple of years I have had before me disputes involving: derivatives—freight rate and currency swaps; the duty owed by forex brokers when closing out a customer's positions; a claim against MasterCard alleging a breach of European competition laws in setting the interchange fee charged to participating merchants; demurrage; challenges to arbitration awards on questions of law and misconduct grounds; claims of sovereign immunity made by Iraq's State Oil Marketing Organisation in resisting enforcement of an arbitration award; anti-suit injunctions; *forum non-conveniens* stay applications; freezing orders.

Shortly before Easter I heard an application for a freezing order made by the US Government against various funds that were alleged to be the proceeds of corruption.[1] The application was made under section 25 of the Civil Jurisdiction and Judgments Act 1982 which empowers the Court to grant interim relief in aid of litigation proceeding in a foreign jurisdiction, whether within the European Union or elsewhere, if it is expedient to do so.

[1] *USA v Mohmd Sani Abacha* [2014] EWHC 993 (Comm).

The foreign proceeding in aid of which the freezing injunction was sought was an *in rem* forfeiture claim brought by the US against certain assets that were alleged to be derived from the proceeds of corrupt misappropriations carried out by the former President of Nigeria, General Abacha, and certain of his relatives and associates. The decision to bring the US claim was in pursuance of the US Kleptocracy Asset Recovery Initiative and was taken with the approval of the US Assistant Attorney General for the Criminal Division.

Part 5 of the Proceeds of Crime Act 2002 (External Requests and Orders) Order 2005 provides a machinery whereby the UK enforcement agency may apply to the Court to enforce an order made by a foreign state against the proceeds of crime. The Strategic Centre for Organised Crime at the Home Office confirmed to the Court that the UK would seek to enforce any civil forfeiture made in the US claim and would return the money recovered to the US on confirmation that the US would in principle seek to return it to the people of Nigeria. However, the UK authorities had refused a request by the US to apply for an interim freezing order under the 2005 Order on the ground that the applicable limitation period of 12 years prevented such an application.

One of the defendants argued that a judgment in the US claim would not be enforceable in England at common law whether *in rem* or *in personam*, and accordingly it could not be expedient to grant the relief sought in aid of the US claim. A judgment in the US claim would not be enforceable *in rem* because the property to be forfeited was outside the US and a judgment *in personam* would not be enforceable at common law because an English court has no jurisdiction to entertain an action for enforcement, either directly or indirectly, of a penal or other public law.

I made a freezing order as requested. The application was not an application to enforce a foreign judgment, but to continue an order designed to hold the ring until a judgment in the US claim could be lawfully enforced under the 2005 Order, and the fact that the application was made by the US in the exercise of its sovereign authority rather than under the 2005 Order was not a reason for concluding that it would be inexpedient to make a freezing injunction. On the contrary, it was expedient to render the assistance sought by the claimant in aid of the US claim. Corruption, like other types of fraud, is a global problem, and it and its consequences are only going to be dealt with effectively if there is cooperation and assistance not only between the governments of states but also between the courts of different national jurisdictions.

Occasionally, a strange fish swims into the net. Recently I was asked to give directions on a claim brought against Crockfords, the London Casino, by a professional gambler for his alleged winnings of seven million pounds at baccarat, to which the defence was that surveillance footage showed that the punter had memorised the printed pattern on the back of the cards, and so knew what was coming out of the shoe. Many commercial transactions, derivatives contracts amongst them, are a form of gambling, but I sent this claim off to be decided in the general list of the Queen's Bench Division.

The Court has its own procedures, specially designed for commercial actions. In particular, it is the judges, and not masters (junior members of the judiciary), who deal with all issues of case management. We do not have a docket system, but a judge can be allocated to a particular case and will then preside over all case management hearings and the trial.

There are 14 judges authorised to sit in the Commercial Court. All will have acquired substantial experience in practice at the Commercial Bar. At any given time, there are eight Commercial judges sitting full time in the Court. The rest are doing other Queen's Bench work, either in London or out on circuit. I shall have something to say about life on circuit a little later.

The Commercial Court cannot afford to over-indulge in self-congratulation. It faces increasing competition from foreign jurisdictions and from arbitration. Its chief curial competitors are the US District Court for the Southern District of New York and the Commercial Division of the NY Supreme Court. There are also some newly emerging challengers, foremost amongst which is the proposed new Singapore International Commercial Court, which will be modelled it seems on the London Commercial Court and manned by specialist Commercial judges not only from Singapore but also other common law jurisdictions. There are also new commercial courts in Dubai and Qatar and a number of civilian jurisdictions in Europe are seeking to enter the fray by allowing proceedings to be conducted in English.

The competition is hotting up. What some might take to be knocking copy has been emerging. I offer three examples. First, in his COMBAR Annual Lecture (2013) the Singapore Chief Justice spoke warmly in favour of Singapore's proposed new International Commercial Court, and suggested that there was a risk of the English commercial common law becoming tainted with alien civilian ideas that could engender uncertainty where the commercial community wants predictability.

Second, the German Federal Minister of Justice has issued a paper entitled 'Law—Made in Germany', in which the Anglo-Saxon common law is disparaged and litigants are encouraged to opt instead for the certainty of the German civil code, which makes no provision for class actions or for awards of punitive damages.

Third, members of two New York law firms, Mr Paul Cohen of Perkins Coie and Ms Gabriella Farina of Thompson & Knight, have published an article in *Global Arbitration Review* entitled: 'Rue Britannia: why English law is a poor choice for international arbitration', in which they boldly assert that compared with US law, English law is irredeemably backward in excluding evidence of negotiations when construing contracts and in adopting an objective approach to the formation of contracts. The authors' ignorance and parochialism is a sad reflection on the New York Bar.

Their names will no doubt have been noted by COMBAR'S blackball committee in the unlikely event they apply to COMBAR for honorary membership.

There will be many reasons why one court rather than another, or arbitration, will be chosen by potential or actual litigants. Cost is bound to be a significant factor. This is something primarily for the profession to worry about, but the judiciary can make a contribution by endorsing the concept of *disclosure lite*, if this be chosen by the parties, and by insisting on much shorter witness statements, pleadings and written arguments.

As to the fees charged by the courts, this is something ultimately in the hands of national governments. In England for the first time in centuries we have a Lord Chancellor and Secretary of State for Justice who is not a lawyer. It is he who has put out to consultation a proposal that the Commercial Court should charge fees at a rate calculated not only to recover the cost of providing the Court, but to make a profit that can go to subsidise other parts of the justice system, such as the criminal courts. The opposition to this proposal has been almost unanimous: the higher judiciary, the judges of the Commercial Court, COMBAR and the London Commercial solicitors have all raised strong objections. We shall know if our views have been heeded later this year.

The Commercial judges reflect the changes that have been going on over the last 30 years in legal education and training. When I came to the Bar, most barristers joining the profession had read law as an undergraduate discipline and then did pupillage with an individual member of the Bar. The pupil/pupil master relationship was personal to the parties thereto. The pupil master's set of chambers would often not be informed of the pupillage until the new pupil's arrival. A pupil master was more or less free to have as many pupils as he wanted.

Nowadays, many entrants to the English Bar are non-law graduates and become excellent lawyers after just a one-year conversion course and a year studying for the Bar exams. And pupillage is greatly changed. Today, the relationship is with the Chambers rather than with any one individual member of the set, and pupils are paid; indeed in the leading commercial sets they are paid extremely well.

Things were very different in 1977. My pupil master was Derry Irvine, Lord Irvine of Lairg, who was Lord Chancellor from 1997 to 2002. He had a brilliant intellect but on first acquaintance he was very frightening. It was like being taken into the depths of a slave galley and ordered to pull ceaselessly on a great oar. After eight years of slack and idle thought in the groves of academe, my hands were pathetically soft. Almost the first words my pupil master addressed to me were: 'Now remember, there's to be nae academic wanking.' I looked along the mighty oar. To my immediate right was a grinning young man who was obviously enjoying my discomfort. His name was Tony Blair. Sitting next to him was an attractive young lady from Liverpool surreptitiously trying to read *Das Kapital* when the Master wasn't looking. Her name was Cherie Booth. We soon became firm friends, as people do who share extreme adversity. It was me, rather than Derry, who played the role of Cupid.

These were pre-designer water days. Derry's pupils quickly got used to consuming prodigious quantities of alcohol in El Vino's, otherwise known as Pomeroy's to devotees of Rumpole of the Bailey. Pupils were not paid, but they never paid for drinks.

In Cherie's autobiography *Speaking for Myself*, she writes that when we were pupils together she asked me under a vow of secrecy to take Tony out on his birthday until 8.00 pm and then to bring him back to her flat where she would be giving him a surprise birthday party. She records that it was well after 11.00 pm that I delivered my charge to her door in a dreadfully unpromising state, by when the party spirit had drained away from the few guests still there. I have no recollection of these events. I have however decided against defamation proceedings. I am also no longer a member of the drinking classes.

As I mentioned earlier, Commercial judges spend part of the year out of London on circuit. The idea of judges travelling around the country to do justice goes back to Norman times. The *Anglo-Saxon Chronicle* tells us that in 1124, the King's Justiciar, Ralph Bassett, descended on Huncote in Leicestershire, and hanged 44 thieves and put out the eyes of six men and deprived them of their testicles. A good early example of zero tolerance.

On circuit, High Court judges stay in houses called lodgings, specially staffed and run to accommodate visiting judges, and it is the longest-serving judge staying there who rules the roost and must be deferred to in all things. Some time ago, a very senior and austere judge was due to sit in Manchester. His Lordship had been divorced more than once, on each occasion for adultery. Upon learning that a newly appointed judge who was a heavy smoker was coming to stay in the Manchester lodgings, the senior judge wrote a letter: 'Dear S, I hear you are an inveterate smoker. Please understand that if you must smoke whilst at the Manchester Lodgings, you will do so in the garden. Yours etc, T.'

Two days later T received the following reply. 'Dear T, thank you for your letter. I understand that you are an inveterate adulterer. If you are going to commit adultery whilst at lodgings, I trust you will do so in the garden. Yours, S.'

In the Commercial Court neither counsel nor the judges are robed. It is very different out on circuit, where when trying crime we wear wigs and robes of scarlet trimmed with ermine. Twenty years ago, the judges would be driven to court already attired in court dress, with a police motorcycle escort. The idea was to impress the populace with the majesty of the law. One morning as the motorcade made its way to Manchester Crown Court an angry citizen threw a brick through the limousine's windscreen. He was promptly arrested and brought before the senior judge to be sentenced for a gross contempt of court. The contemnor said he was very sorry, he had meant no offence to the judges. He had thought he was aiming at the Lord Mayor. He was let off with a conditional discharge.

On another occasion, also in Manchester, Mr Justice Bernard Caulfield was staying in the Manchester lodgings with Mr Justice Pat Russell. One evening, Caulfield J was stopped by an officious policeman as he drove in ordinary clothes back to the lodgings. The conversation went as follows:

> Policeman: 'I'm PC Brown. Who are you, Sonny Jim, and where, Sonny Jim, are you going? I want to see your licence and your insurance certificate.'
>
> Caulfield J: 'I do not have on me my licence or insurance. My name is Bernard and I am staying in lodgings with my friend Pat.'
>
> Policeman: 'Well, listen to me Sonny Jim, you are to report at the police station tomorrow before 9.30 pm with your licence and insurance certificate. You'll be in serious trouble if do you not show up.'

The next morning, fully robed, Caulfield J was driven to the police station on the way to court. When His Lordship was asked by the desk sergeant what he could do for him, Caulfield J said: 'Tell PC Brown that Sonny Jim is here.'

Commercial judges often serve as Presiding Judge on one of the six circuits of England and Wales. I was myself Presiding Judge on the Western Circuit. There is a considerable ceremonial side to a Presiding Judge's life, which requires him or her, amongst other things, to attend numerous church services throughout the year, when the Almighty is asked to help in making the judges wise and merciful. On these occasions the judge wears the full ceremonial kit of a scarlet robe with ermine hood, full bottom wig, breeches, and tights purchased from Mothercare. I remember in preparation for the service at Exeter Cathedral pulling on my tights in a room above an Anne Summers' sex shop in the company of 20 other judges all doing the same. Always in attendance at these services is the High Sheriff of the county in question, dressed in velvet breeches and wearing his sword of office. Dorchester parish church on the Western Circuit is a small place of worship, with very narrow pews. The High Sheriff of Dorset, a man of some girth, was there for the annual Dorchester service with his sword swinging at his side. As the congregation stood to sing a hymn, the hilt of the Sheriff's sword snagged on the edge of the pew. There was a horrible ripping sound as the Sheriffs' breeches were torn asunder. There he stood, speechless and breechless, in Gaza. It did not assuage his embarrassment that the hymn he was rising to sing was 'Stand up, Stand up for Jesus'.

It has reached that time when it is well to recall what happened as Voltaire lay dying. A priest had been sent for, who said to Voltaire: 'Monsieur, I urge you to renounce the devil', to which Voltaire replied: 'Now, my Good Man, is not a time to make enemies.'

11

Deference or Difference? The Relationship Between English and International Courts and Tribunals

PROFESSOR JAMES CRAWFORD AC, SC, FBA

James Crawford AC, SC, FBA is the Whewell Professor of International Law at the University of Cambridge, and holder of a Research Chair at La Trobe University in Melbourne. He has previously been Professor of International Law at the Universities of Adelaide and Sydney. Professor Crawford delivered the COMBAR Annual Lecture in November 2014 at Middle Temple Hall. At the time of the lecture, he was about to be elected as a Judge of the International Court of Justice (ICJ) by the United Nations General Assembly and Security Council.

IN AN ARBITRATION last week presided over by Lord Collins, the counsel on the other side said of an argument I'd made, which distinguished between jurisdiction and application law, that I was behaving like a private international lawyer. This was not perhaps the best thing to say before Lord Collins. But I responded by saying 'thank you for the compliment'. When my students ask me 'how did I become an international lawyer', there is a short answer. You become a lawyer first. Many people are still under the illusion that it is possible to be an international lawyer without being a lawyer. I think that's wrong, and I've dedicated my career to trying to show it is wrong. I hope to do the same in translation.

It is a quarter-century since the Commercial Bar Association was founded, in 1989. In a decision reported that year, part of the *Tin Council* litigation, the Court of Appeal observed that although an authority on non-justiciability seemed to suggest that English courts could not examine issues of international law, that view could not be right, since 'the English courts are often examining issues of international law'.[1] Well, that 'often' has turned into 'very much more often', in terms of the developments that have occurred in the succeeding 25 years.

[1] *Maclaine Watson & Co Ltd v International Tin Council* [1989] 1 Ch 253, 264.

Many developments have contributed to this. Although investor–state arbitration clauses began to appear in bilateral investment treaties—the very first was in 1959—as late as 1980 no case under such a clause had been decided. The number now is in excess of 400. The first was decided in 1990.[2] Now such arbitrations are frequent, and they are frequently connected with domestic law and litigation. In *Occidental v Ecuador*, the Court of Appeal held that an award made in favour of the appellant under a bilateral investment treaty between the US and Ecuador gave rise to justiciable rights in the United Kingdom, pursuant to provisions of the Arbitration Act, even though the treaty was, not surprisingly, not part of English law.[3] During the same period, the Human Rights Act has incorporated the European Convention on Human Rights, at least up to a point. 'Up to a point, Lord Copper', as Evelyn Waugh would have said. Doctrine on what is and is not justiciable has developed to an extent where it seems unreal even to suggest that English courts cannot examine issues of international law. Sir Robert Jennings—one of my predecessors in the Whewell Chair, and on the Court, once called it 'a quiet and often unnoticed revolution' by which 'the old well defined boundaries between public international law, private international law and municipal law are no longer boundaries but grey areas'.[4]

So if a quarter-century ago it would have seemed strange—indeed, very strange—for a public international lawyer to give this annual lecture, today I hope it does not. I want to talk about those 'grey areas', to discuss deference between international courts and tribunals, on one side, and English courts on the other.

The International and the Domestic as Interpenetrating Legal Orders

What makes the question of deference significant is that neither side, neither English law nor international law, is inherently subordinate to the other. At least that is the prevailing view, although there is some dissent among scholars. Hans Kelsen asserted that the authority of domestic law was delegated from international law, a distinctly arid and a priori proposition.[5] That might be an attractive theory for an international lawyer not wanting to be a lawyer, but to say that before an English court would not get you very far.

[2] *Asian Agricultural Products Ltd v Sri Lanka*, Final Award, ICSID Case No ARB/87/3; II18 (1990). See N Blackaby et al, *Redfern and Hunter on International Arbitration* (Oxford, OUP, 2009) [8.08]–[8.11].

[3] *Occidental Exploration & Production Co v Ecuador* [2006] QB 432, 457.

[4] RY Jennings, 'The judiciary, international and national, and the development of international law' (1996) 45 *International Comparative Law Quarterly* 1.

[5] H Kelsen, *Das Problem der Souveränität und die Theorie des Völkerrechts-Beitrag zu einer reinen Rechtslehre* (JC Mohr, 1920); H Kelsen, *Reine Rechtslehre: Einleitung in die rechtswissenschaftliche Problematik* (Deuticke, 1934); J von Bernstorff, *The Public International Law Theory of Hans Kelsen: Believing in Universal Law* (Cambridge, CUP, 2010).

The reality is that the domestic system of each state dictates the terms on which international law enters into that system. If there is a sense in which international law delegates authority, it does so in a completely formal rather than a substantive way. In any event, international law demands from states and their institutions only a particular result, as a general matter; it is for each state to determine how it achieves that result, in accordance with its constitutional arrangements. This gives rise to the spectre, which we have seen in real life on a number of occasions recently, where federal constitutional courts, or national constitutional courts, are in effect declining to apply international decisions on constitutional grounds—as the Italian constitutional court did last month in relation to the unanimous decision of the International Court in the *Germany v Italy* case on state immunity.[6]

On the one hand, I want to defend the idea that each system has, to use a terrible German phrase, *Kompetenz-kompetenz* in relation to the issue, and on the other hand to defend the idea that resolution is possible, and there is continuing tension between those two ideas, as we will see from some of the cases.

But a better way to think about international and national law is as interpenetrating legal systems. 'Each system is supreme *in its own field*; neither has hegemony over the other': I am quoting the 8th edition of Brownlie's *Principles*,[7] with permission. The passage is the same in the 7th edition, you will be relieved to hear.[8] In accordance with this basic principle, English law dictates the terms on which international law enters into English law. It is worthwhile stressing that these terms take the form of common law rules, not rules of international law—though they are *about* international law, or at least about international transactions. Americans call them foreign relations law. Each of the common law rules can be set against different, sometimes even contradictory rules of international law. They are common law rules of recognition, of reception or non-reception. Each legal system by definition has its own rules of recognition or reception: that is what it is to be a legal system.

Now, I don't to this audience need to go into detail about the relevant English rules of reception, but I will summarise them briefly. One distinction from many civil law systems is how English law deals with treaties, on the basis of the fundamental proposition that the executive has no legislative authority, no power to change the law by making promises to other states. That does not mean that unimplemented treaties have no relevance domestically. That was true even before the Human Rights Act came into force, as

[6] *Jurisdictional Immunities of the State (Germany v Italy: Greece intervening)* [2012] ICJ 99.

[7] J Crawford, *Brownlie's Principles of Public International Law*, 8th edn (Oxford, OUP, 2012) 110.

[8] I Brownlie, *Principles of Public International Law*, 7th edn (Oxford, OUP, 2008) 53: 'Each system is supreme *in its own field*, and neither has a hegemony over the other'.

far as concerned the European Convention,[9] and it is true now in relation to other conventions. It has also been held that where a public authority gives reasons for a decision based on a treaty provision, the courts can review that decision by reference to the correctness of those reasons, at least up to the level of *Wednesbury* unreasonableness.[10]

In a more complex way, the role of customary international law in English law—customary international law can be compendiously described as the rest of international law apart from treaties, and it might be better if the description stopped there—the often-articulated rule is that customary international law is itself part of the law of England, a rule that goes back to the eighteenth century and to Lord Mansfield.[11] In *Chung Chi Cheung*, Lord Atkin, one of the greatest English judges of the twentieth century, observed that '[o]n any judicial issue [the Courts] seek to ascertain what the rule is, and, having found it, they will treat it as incorporated into the domestic law, so far as it is not inconsistent with rules enacted by statutes or finally declared by their tribunals'.[12] The standard modern authority of *Trendtex*, in the Court of Appeal, is to the same effect.[13]

There is some debate about whether the phrase 'part of' is an accurate formulation. We might say that the law of torts or restitution is 'part of' the law, but we would be talking about issues of internal classification, not relations with another system. As Lord Bingham preferred to describe it, international law is a 'source' of English law.[14] I am not sure that the word 'source' is any more helpful; it replaces one uncertain term with another. How we characterise the relationship may be little more than a difference in emphasis. The point is that the rule depends on a rule of English law empowering the judiciary to apply international law in appropriate cases, and the situation might vary from one case to another.

There are four elements to that basic proposition. The first is that the English courts acknowledge the existence of a body of international law whose content is a matter for argument, not evidence. Counsel argue international law like they argue English law, on the basis of authority—using, I hope, *Brownlie's Principles of International Law*, 8th edition. Unlike foreign law, international law is not presumed to be the same as the English common law in any sense: it is a matter for legal argument. The courts

[9] Eg, *R v Chief Immigration Officer, Heathrow Airport; Ex parte Salamat Bibi* [1976] 1 WLR 979, 984; *Gleaves v Deakin* [1980] AC 477. Contra: *Malone v Metropolitan Police Commissioner* [1979] Ch 344, 379.

[10] *Wednesbury Corporation v Ministry of Housing and Local Government (No 2)* [1965] 3 All ER 571.

[11] *Buvot v Barbuit* (1737) Cases t Talbot 281; *Triquet v Bath* (1764) 3 Burr 1478; *Heathfield v Chilton* (1767) 4 Burr 2015; *Viveash v Becker* (1814) 3 M & S 284.

[12] *Chung Chi Cheung v The King* [1939] AC 160, 167–68.

[13] *Trendtex Trading Corp v Central Bank of Nigeria* [1977] QB 529, 554.

[14] *R v Jones (Margaret)* [2002] 2 All ER 741, 751 [11].

determine for themselves what international law is, and in that sense they are taken to know the law.

Secondly, the courts can in appropriate cases apply international law as the rule of decision, or apply it as an aspect of the policy of the law—as public policy—as they did in *Oppenheimer v Cattermole*.[15]

Thirdly, on matters on which international law has something to say, legislation should if possible be presumed to be consistent with it.[16]

The final element is that the rules of international law are taken 'as existing from time to time', a proposition for which *Trendtex* is authority.[17] If a rule of international law changes, then it should be the changed rule that is taken into English law, not the old rule. There would be no point in English law adhering to a proposition of international law which was no longer accepted—though there must be a presumption against change; it doesn't change on a daily basis. This illustrates the notion of interpenetrating legal systems: the rule retains its character as a rule of international law despite its incorporation into the common law.

There is one other rule that forms part of the background against which we should consider questions of deference. This is the principle of non-justiciability. The key case, of course, is *Buttes Gas & Oil*.[18] Lord Wilberforce, another great judge of the twentieth century, articulated the act of state doctrine as something which had always been part of English law, despite the absence of recent authority. He explained the various versions of it: the domestic act of state doctrine, the international act of state doctrine. He described it as a principle of 'judicial restraint or abstention', one which 'is inherent in the very nature of the judicial process',[19] by which he meant the national or (as international lawyers quaintly call it) the municipal judicial process.

Now that 'general principle' has a long pedigree; it goes back to the seventeenth century. And it is applied not because the adjudication on a particular issue will be a source of embarrassment in foreign relations—embarrassment is not a good basis for a rule of English law; the judges are not often embarrassed. It is said that it is applied because it is inherent in the limited capacity of a domestic court, an insight which Lord Wilberforce, who appeared before the International Court early in his career, was well qualified to reach. He wasn't saying that there was 'a judicial no-man's-land'

[15] *Oppenheimer v Cattermole* [1975] 1 All ER 538.

[16] *R v Jones (Margaret)* [2006] 2 All ER 741.

[17] *Trendtex Trading Corp v Central Bank of Nigeria* [1977] QB 529, 554.

[18] *Buttes Gas & Oil Corp v Hammer (No 3)* [1982] AC 888. See my case note at J Crawford, 'Case No 2 *Buttes Gas and Oil Co v Hammer and another (Nos 2 & 3)*; *Occidental Petroleum and another v Buttes Gas and Oil Co and another (Nos 1 and 2)*' (1982) 53 *British Yearbook of International Law* 259.

[19] *Buttes Gas & Oil Corp v Hammer (No 3)* [1982] AC 888, 931.

in all cases, but he was saying that there is an area which, for example, in the context of international boundary disputes, is a no-man's-land so far as domestic, municipal or national courts are concerned.[20]

But no-man's-land does shift occasionally, after the most recent offensive, when one side or the other gains ground, even if it is seldom and even if it is seldom very much ground. The general principle of non-justiciability has been revealed to be not as 'general' as it sounds. It is confined to acts very much within the territory of the foreign state, and possibly to disputes about the extent of the territory of the foreign state.[21] It does not confer immunity on a state's commercial activities.[22] It does not apply to foreign acts of state that are in breach of clearly established rules of international law, as the House of Lords held in *Kuwait Airways*, or contrary to English principles of public policy, as it held equally in that case.[23] '[C]onceptions of public policy', as the House of Lords said, 'should move with the times'.[24]

There are limits to this in commercial contexts. Although the English principles of public policy identified in *Kuwait Airways* may embrace flagrant breaches of human rights, the expropriation in *Kuwait Airways* was a special case achieved through an unlawful use of force—internationally unlawful as determined by the Security Council. English courts have not recognised expropriation without compensation as being in breach of clearly established international norms.[25] Nor did the American Supreme Court, until corrected by legislation.

To summarise: although neither international law nor the English legal system has hegemony over the other, and each is supreme in its own field, their relations are nonetheless rule-governed: the international legal system enters into the common law through the rules on the incorporation of treaties and customary international law and the rule of non-justiciability, qualified and restricted as it now is.

The Possible Binding Effect of International Decisions in English Courts

Now, I turn from that general summary to the position of deference if a court in one system is confronted with a decision of another.

The first thing that occurs to a lawyer in that situation is the possibility that the other decision may be binding in its own terms or on the parties

[20] ibid, 938.
[21] *Yukos Capital v OJSC Rosneft Oil* [2014] QB 458, [66].
[22] ibid, [92]–[94].
[23] *Kuwait Airways Corporation v Iraqi Airways Case (Nos 4 & 5)* [2002] 2 AC 883.
[24] *Blathwayt v Baron Cawley* [1976] AC 397, 426 (Lord Wilberforce), quoted in *Kuwait Airways Corporation v Iraqi Airways Case (Nos 4 & 5)* [2002] 2 AC 883, [28] (Lord Nicholls).
[25] *Yukos Capital v OJSC Rosneft Oil* [2014] QB 458, [72].

to the litigation by virtue of *res judicata* or issue estoppel. There are certainly some situations where this is so—for example, most obviously, ICSID awards under the 1965 Washington Convention, which cannot be reviewed by domestic courts and are to be treated as final decisions of the highest national court and enforced as such.[26] So they have *res judicata* effect.[27]

A more interesting example is *Dallal v Bank Mellat*, which concerned a decision of the Iran–US Claims Tribunal, established after the hostage crisis. The Algiers Accord was not part of English law, of course, but curiously it wasn't part of Dutch law either; it hadn't been implemented in Dutch law. Dallal lost a case involving a claim on a cheque before the Iran–US Claims Tribunal, in circumstances where, Mr Justice Hobhouse held, the judgment was not enforceable in the law of the Netherlands and therefore not enforceable as such in English law.[28] But he went on to strike out the cause of action on the grounds of issue estoppel, because it was decided by 'a court of competent jurisdiction'.[29] '[T]he competence of a tribunal', he held, 'can be looked for and found in international law and practice'; '[i]f under international law such a tribunal is competent, its competence ought to be recognised by the English courts'.[30] It did not matter that the Tribunal had decided the issue as a matter of the burden of proof, and in what strikes an English lawyer as an idiosyncratic manner: there is still a determination which gives rise to an issue estoppel,[31] unless there are some 'special circumstances' which make it 'unjust or inappropriate to apply the principle'.[32]

But there are reasons why *res judicata* and issue estoppel will not commonly be applicable in relation to international decisions. The House of Lords recognised this in *Lyons*,[33] in which an application was brought to quash convictions following a Strasbourg decision that the evidence used against the accused had infringed their rights—their right not to incriminate themselves—under the European Convention. Noting that applicable legislation provided that the convictions could only be quashed if they were deemed 'unsafe', Lord Bingham held that *Dallal* did not assist the applicants, 'since in that case Hobhouse J was free to apply familiar common law principles unconstrained by any statutory enactment'.[34] Lord Millett

[26] Convention on the Settlement of Investment Disputes between States and Nationals of Other States (1965) 575 UNTS 19, art 53(1).
[27] C Schreuer, *The ICSID Convention: A Commentary* (Cambridge, CUP, 2009) 1136.
[28] *Dallal v Bank Mellat* [1986] QB 441.
[29] ibid, 454–55.
[30] ibid, 460.
[31] ibid, 455.
[32] ibid, 454–55.
[33] *R v Lyons* [2002] UKHL 44.
[34] ibid, [19] (Lord Bingham).

commented that even if *res judicata* were applicable, 'the present case is one where the court would be constrained by statute to disapply it'.[35]

Finally I should say a few words about how the principles of *res judicata* and issue estoppel are perceived by international courts and tribunals. In the context of international law, *res judicata* is inclusive of issue estoppel; the distinctions that English law has drawn are not drawn.[36] In *Apotex v United States*, a NAFTA tribunal held that a Canadian pharmaceutical company could not re-litigate the question of whether new drug applications made in the United States constituted 'investments' for the purposes of Chapter 11 of NAFTA, given that a previous tribunal had decided that they did not constitute 'investments' for the purposes of NAFTA, so there was a *res judicata*—we would call it an issue estoppel in relation to that situation.[37]

When the problem was considered by the Committee on Commercial Arbitration of the International Law Association in 2006, it decided not to include in its recommendation a requirement that *res judicata* apply only within the international legal order, '[i]n order not to prejudge further developments'. The Committee concluded 'that a process of permeation and interaction between different legal orders' was 'only beginning and may result in the legal community no longer viewing private law and public law as operating in separate legal orders'.[38]

Against this background, I want to turn to some recent cases of deference—or lack of deference—by domestic courts to international courts and tribunals in questions of international law. It is too early to form a general theory of what's going on, except that what's going on is the subject of considerable change. The influence of human rights and refugee protection is strong. There are also cases under the Human Rights Act, as it still is, in which—for example, *Al Jedda*—activities of the United Kingdom abroad are subject to what appear to be European disciplines.[39] There's no time to discuss all the issues here.

Deference Consistent with the Act of State Doctrine

I want to start with the act of state doctrine as it has been explained in two important recent decisions, *Yukos*[40] and *Belhaj*.[41] I start with *Yukos*. The

35 ibid, [107] (Lord Millett).

36 J Crawford, *Brownlie's Principles of Public International Law*, 8th edn (Oxford, OUP, 2012) 61.

37 *Apotext Holdings Inc and Apotex Inc v United States*, Award, ICSID Case No ARB(AF)/12/1 (JR Crook, JW Rowley & VV Veeder), 25 August 2014, [7.51].

38 ILA Committee on Commercial Arbitration, *Recommendation 3*(40) (Toronto, 2006).

39 *R (Al-Jedda) v Secretary of State for Defence* [2008] 2 WLR 31.

40 *Yukos Capital v OJSC Rosneft Oil* [2014] QB 458.

41 *Belhaj v Straw* [2013] EWHC 4111 (High Court); [2014] EWCA Civ 1394 (Court of Appeal).

facts are unusual, but the case illustrates issues raised by the interaction of an English court with an arbitral tribunal acting under the ICC rules, and with foreign domestic courts. You know in general about the *Yukos* controversy, which spawned a great deal of litigation. A Russian court set the awards aside, a decision which was ignored by the appellate court in the Netherlands, on the grounds of partiality and executive domination. A further enforcement action was brought in England. The Court of Appeal said that the act of state doctrine did not preclude inquiry into the substantive justice available in the Russian courts. Far from it: the Court held that 'subject to the requirements of any treaty or convention, an English court must *always* be entitled to ask and adjudicate on the issue whether a foreign court decision should or should not be recognised or enforced'.[42] The act of state doctrine is qualified by reference to judicial decisions accordingly; judicial decisions, those decisions of organs of the state, are not benefited by the act of state doctrine.

The Court, in a graphic simile, said:

> The important thing is to recognise that increasingly in the modern world the [act of state] doctrine is being defined, like a silhouette, by its limitations, rather than to regard it as occupying the whole ground save to the extent that an exception can be imposed.[43]

(A position which, I interpolate, you might have thought applied as a result of Lord Wilberforce's rather sweeping statements in *Buttes Oil & Gas*.) The Court in *Yukos* continued:

> That ... would explain why it has become wholly commonplace to adjudicate upon or call into question the acts of a foreign state in relation to matters of international convention, whether it is the persecution of applicant asylum refugees, or the application of the Rome Statute with regard to international criminal responsibility or other matters ...
>
> It ... has to be remembered that the [act of state] doctrine was first developed in an era which predated the existence of modern international human rights law. The idea that the rights of a state might be curtailed by its obligations in the field of human rights would have seemed somewhat strange in that era.[44]

That echoes Lord Nicholls' remark in *Kuwait Airways* that '[a]s nations become ever more interdependent, the need to recognise and adhere to standards of conduct set by international law becomes ever more important'.[45] In other words: hold states to what they say, not what they (or some of them) do.

42 *Yukos Capital v OJSC Rosneft Oil* [2014] QB 458, [125]. Emphasis added.
43 ibid, [115].
44 ibid.
45 *Kuwait Airways Corporation v Iraqi Airways Case (Nos 4 & 5)* [2002] 2 AC 883, [28].

It is not as if English courts have simply stormed into the 'judicial no-man's-land' of *Buttes Oil* and planted the national flag on previously unclaimed ground. Their willingness to adjudicate such matters has been accompanied by a willingness to defer to international standards, including international human rights standards; it is holding governments to these standards which they profess. The Court spoke of deference in this way: it described the standards by which the Russian court was to be measured as 'what is more and more being expressed as a global deference to the rule of law', not a deference to sovereignty as such, but a deference to a sovereignty qualified by the standards of the rule of law.[46] In this respect, *Yukos* symbolises an inclination *towards* deference to international standards, and away from the deference to sovereignty in its naked form.

Belhaj v Straw, of equal importance, was decided by a strong Court of Appeal in October 2014.[47] The claimants were a member of the Libyan opposition and his wife. They sought asylum in the United Kingdom and were the subjects of alleged serious maltreatment in a variety of countries—China, Malaysia, Thailand, Libya itself—and on board a US-registered aircraft.[48]

Mr Justice Simon found that the act of state doctrine *did* operate as a bar to the claim. He couldn't, he said, enquire into the acts of this range of sovereigns in the circumstances. But the point was overturned by the Court of Appeal. The application of the doctrine hinged on two matters. First, there is the *Kirkpatrick* limitation:[49] that the act of state doctrine applies when a court is asked to adjudicate on the legal effect, or validity, of an act of state, and not on the facts which occurred. The act of state doctrine, in short, only applies when the question is one of legal validity or consequences; the courts are free to determine the facts of a case and to do so in accordance with ordinary evidentiary procedures. The *Kirkpatrick* exception didn't apply in this case, because evidently the appellants sought review of the legal effect of their treatment.

Secondly and more importantly, there was the public policy exception. The difficulty for the claimants was on what basis it could be said that their detention was unlawful. They sought to rely on the presumption that the law of the states concerned was the same as English law, but both Mr Justice Simon in the High Court rejected that presumption as 'unreal'.[50] Instead the Court of Appeal emphasised that the conceptions of public policy should

[46] *Yukos Capital v OJSC Rosneft Oil* [2014] QB 458, [90].

[47] *Belhaj v Straw* [2013] EWHC 4111 (High Court); [2014] EWCA Civ 1394 (Court of Appeal).

[48] ibid, [19]–[20].

[49] *Kirkpatrick v Environmental Tectonics Corp International* 493 US 400 (1990). See also: *Yukos Capital v OJSC Rosneft Oil* [2014] QB 458, [95]–[112].

[50] *Belhaj v Straw* [2013] EWHC 4111, [140(c)], [142].

move in accordance with developments of international law. 'A fundamental change', the Court said 'has occurred within public international law. The traditional view of public international law as a system of law merely regulating the conduct of states among themselves on the international plane has long been discarded. In its place has emerged a system which includes the regulation of human rights by international law, a system of which individuals are rightly considered to be subjects.[51]

(Rather dramatic words, coming from the Court of Appeal.)

> A corresponding shift in international public policy has also taken place… These changes have been reflected in a growing willingness on the part of courts in this jurisdiction [that is, England] to address and investigate the conduct of foreign states and issues of public international law when appropriate.[52]

So a considerable transformation has occurred from the broad statement of Lord Wilberforce in *Buttes Oil & Gas* that the courts cannot adjudicate on the transactions of foreign sovereign states, to a much more qualified doctrine which leaves some but not much scope for act of state. We shall see how the case fares in the Supreme Court, of course, because it is subject to appeal.

How much of the doctrine will remain if courts are left to determine its application on the basis of a wide-ranging public policy exception remains to be seen. In *Yukos*, the Court had already recognised that the emergence of international human rights law subsequent to the development of the act of state doctrine had strengthened the idea that the rights of a state might be curtailed by its obligations to individuals.[53] *Belhaj v Straw* in the Court of Appeal confirms that position. The Court similarly found that there was no 'lack of judicial or manageable standards'—another one of Lord Wilberforce's rubrics—'[o]n the contrary, the applicable principles of international law and English law are clearly established'.[54]

Deference to a Decision of an International Tribunal

In recent times we've seen a level of deference by English courts to international decisions, which might be thought even to be exaggerated.

I refer, for example, to *A v Secretary of State for the Home Department (No 2)*,[55] the decision of 2006, another human rights case of course. The question was whether evidence allegedly obtained by torture could be taken

[51] ibid, [115].
[52] ibid.
[53] *Yukos Capital v OJSC Rosneft Oil* [2014] QB 458, [115].
[54] *Belhaj v Straw* [2014] EWCA Civ 1394, [118].
[55] *A v Secretary of State for the Home Department (No 2)* [2006] 2 AC 221.

into account in determining a question before the Special Immigration Appeals Commission. In his leading speech, Lord Bingham found that the European Convention was to be interpreted not in a vacuum but taking account of other international obligations.[56] In particular the prohibition of torture enjoyed the highest normative force recognised by international law.[57] And Lord Bingham leant heavily on a decision of the International Criminal Tribunal for the former Yugoslavia in *Furundzija*,[58] which he described as having 'fully and authoritatively explained' the implications of 'the *jus cogens* nature of the international crime of torture'.[59]

Of course, in *Furundzija*, the tribunal was concerned with criminal responsibility, not with civil responsibility, and what it said about the peremptory character of the prohibition on torture has to be read in that context. But the premise underlying the *Furundzija* case is that a violation of a peremptory norm of international law has a direct effect on the legal character and consequences of domestic legislative, administrative or judicial acts relating to the violation.

It is possible to disagree with Lord Bingham's comment that *Furundzija* 'fully and authoritatively explained' the implications of *jus cogens* norms,[60] especially since the International Court has been rather resolute in declining to take into account the *jus cogens* or peremptory status of norms at the level of jurisdiction, most notably in *Germany v Italy*.[61] In fact no attempt has yet been made to work out what the consequences of the peremptory status of norms would be. So there is a danger, even for as significant a judge as Lord Bingham, in taking individual decisions and treating them as canonical in an area where the law is changing rather rapidly. Lord Bingham was nonetheless willing to defer to the explanation of the tribunal in *Furundzija*, despite the fact that the International Court has subsequently qualified it.

The International Court's decision in the *Wall* case has been cited a number of times in the United Kingdom courts, but not always with the same unreflective deference. In *R (Mohamed) v Secretary of State for Foreign and Commonwealth Affairs*,[62] the High Court reconsidered what Lord Bingham said in *A (No 2)*. It also reviewed a much longer list of British and international authorities relevant to the legal consequences of a breach of a *jus cogens* or peremptory norm. It observed correctly that none of them

[56] ibid, [28]–[29].

[57] ibid, [30]–[33].

[58] *Prosecutor v Furundzija*, 10 December 1998, International Criminal Tribunal for the Former Yugoslavia, Case No IT-98–17/T 10.

[59] *A v Secretary of State for the Home Department (No 2)* [2006] 2 AC 221, [33].

[60] ibid, [33].

[61] *Jurisdictional Immunities of the State (Germany v Italy: Greece intervening)* [2012] ICJ 99.

[62] *R (Mohamed) v Secretary of State for Foreign and Commonwealth Affairs* [2008] EWHC 2048 (Admin).

'purports to provide a comprehensive statement of the legal consequences flowing from the [peremptory] status of the primary rule'.[63]

Now, the courts are not being assisted in pursuing these issues, in cases involving torture and analogous problems, by the absence of articulated guidance from international courts. Even the *Germany v Italy* case, which is exceptionally well-reasoned by the Court's standards—and I think it is fair to say by *any* standards—still doesn't explain in much depth why it is that peremptory norms don't have the effect you would expect them to have if they are to be treated as seriously as everyone says they should be. Perhaps if the English courts had been able to point to a more articulated version of the doctrine by the International Court, some of these problems might have been avoided.

Deference in the Context of Human Rights

I turn to deference in the context of human rights, a subject of great controversy now, given the current government's adumbrations in relation to the future of the Human Rights Act. In some cases it may be more accurate to speak of dialogue rather than deference, and that's certainly true in relation to the dialogue between the European Court of Human Rights and the English courts, especially the Supreme Court.

For example, the first *Al-Khawaja* decision was given by the Fourth Section of the European Court in 2009, finding that the United Kingdom had breached two paragraphs of Article 6 of the European Convention—the fair trial guarantee and the right of an accused to examine witnesses.[64] The case was referred to the Grand Chamber for further consideration.

In the meantime, the United Kingdom Supreme Court took the opportunity to reconsider the issue in *Horncastle*. It declined to follow the European Court of Human Rights and held that a conviction in the circumstances did not necessarily infringe the relevant paragraphs of Article 6. Lord Phillips made the point that although the requirements under the Human Rights Act to 'take into account' the Strasbourg jurisprudence would normally result in the Supreme Court applying the same principles, on some occasions the Court may have 'concerns as to whether a decision of the Strasbourg court sufficiently appreciates or accommodates particular aspects of our domestic process'.[65] The English hearsay rules, supplemented by statute, had developed over time into a regime with safeguards that rendered the 'sole or decisive' test both unnecessary and prone to severe practical difficulties.

[63] ibid, [179].
[64] *Al-Khawaja and Tahery v UK* App no 26766/05 (ECtHR, 20 January 2009).
[65] *R v Horncastle; R v Marquis* [2010] 2 WLR 47 (SC), 97.

The Court criticised this test as applied by the European Court of Human Rights as arbitrary.

In the event, Strasbourg took the hint. In 2011, in the Grand Chamber in *Al-Khawaja*, it accepted that where hearsay evidence is the sole decisive evidence against the accused, its admission as evidence will not automatically result in a breach of the fair trial guarantee, given other procedural safeguards of English law.[66]

So that's an example of dialogue, where the domestic court has regard to what an international court has said, but doesn't automatically defer to it. After what I said about the interpenetrating character of legal norms, it seems to me that that is entirely appropriate. International courts will earn deference if they deserve it, not merely by virtue of their status. I do not except the International Court of Justice; I think the Court is subject to the same rules as everyone else. Deference is something which is due not by reason of status alone, though status matters, but also by reason of the cogency of the reasoning, and some decisions of the European Court of Human Rights, to single them out, lack cogency. And it is appropriate for national courts to say that.

This leads to an untidy situation, in which each court is the master of its own law. It should act openly and with the knowledge of what's going on in the other relevant forum. It follows that there are no absolute rules, but as Sir Robert Jennings said, 'grey areas'.

The Other Side of the Equation

Now, that is, as it were, one side of the equation. There is another side, which is reflected in a number of recent decisions in which national courts and special constitutional courts are in effect asserting what must be described as a partisan view of the relevant law, as against international decisions. There are examples in Colombia, which I won't discuss for professional reasons, and in particular the recent decision of the Italian constitutional court in the *Germany v Italy* case. That creates a situation in which there is a stand-off which hasn't been resolved, and the resolution of which seems extremely difficult without international conflict.

I don't want to comment on the detail of the *Germany v Italy* case, but I would make the remark that Article 6 and its domestic equivalents—Article 6 of the European Convention, the access to a court requirement—is perhaps difficult to apply in circumstances where the issue is that of immunity or non-justiciability. The question is not just access to a court, but

[66] *Al-Khawaja and Tahery v UK*, ECtHR, App no 26766/05, Grand Chamber, 15 December 2011, [147].

access to *which* court, and on what terms, and although domestic courts may assert that access to *their* jurisdiction is required by their constitution, that can't be true except in a system of universal civil jurisdiction, which we do not have. So the barriers in the way the resolution of conflicts of that sort in a system of interpenetration are real ones. It can't be said that, just because national courts have *Kompetenz-kompetenz*, have authority to determine these questions themselves, their power to do so is unfettered.

The same point might be made about the Court of Justice of the European Union in its decision in *Kadi*.[67] This was not a case of deference to an international court, but of deference to the Security Council. And again there are important questions about how such decisions, which can be understood in due process terms, can be squared with the need for the world to actually deal with the underlying problems. I don't want to criticise *Kadi*—I was counsel for Kadi in the European Court of Justice, and so it seems to me an admirable decision on that ground alone. But it does present a problem. If constitutional courts and quasi-constitutional courts have the last word, there is still the problem that international law has to be complied with, and the modalities for compliance are made unnecessarily complicated by decisions which find what may thought to be an insecure footing in terms such as Article 6, access to justice. Whose justice, where, and when, are not questions which Article 6 itself determines.

Conclusion

Let me conclude. The 'quiet and often unnoticed revolution' that Robert Jennings drew attention to as long ago as 1996[68] has continued to transform the interaction between domestic and international courts, including in commercial cases. This can be seen in the United Kingdom in particular in the greater ease in the handling of international materials—the *Belhaj* court is a marvellous example of that—and the more frequent reference to international standards. Indeed, the application of the act of state doctrine effectively turns on the existence of judicial or manageable standards, and since *Kuwait Airways*, these have often been found in international rules and materials.[69] *Yukos* and *Belhaj v Straw* illustrated this powerfully, and *Belhaj* also suggests that international human rights law is building pressure to limit the application of the act of state doctrine. *A (No 2)* illustrates

[67] Case C-402/05 P *Kadi v Council of the European Union* [2009] 1 AC 1225 (ECJ); Joined Cases C-584/10 P, C-593/10 P and C-595/10 P *Commission, Council, United Kingdom v Kadi* (ECJ, Judgment, 18 July 2013).

[68] RY Jennings, 'The judiciary, international and national, and the development of international law' (1996) 45 *International Comparative Law Quarterly* 1.

[69] *Kuwait Airways Corporation v Iraqi Airways Case (Nos 4 & 5)* [2002] 2 AC 883.

a related development: the increasing willingness of English courts to treat decisions by international courts and tribunals as authoritative, insofar as they deal with particular issues of relevance to the English courts. But there is always a question of translation, of taking the international decision and making it relevant to the issue before the domestic courts. And that issue can't be elided by respect; it can't be elided by deference: it requires further legal analysis.

At the same time as English courts have shifted away from the sort of deference that might previously have caused them to shy away from deciding international questions, they are deferring to an appropriate degree, I would say, to international standards and decisions. And developments at the level of international law in are running in parallel to this: *Al-Khawaja* is a remarkable instance of dialogue between a domestic court and an international court, and deference to the firmer position of a domestic court in assessing whether an international standard has been met. I could have cited other examples, such as *Jones*, in the House of Lords and the European Court of Human Rights.[70] So we are in a situation of dialogue, rather than of categories. The grey areas are grey areas which need exploration, and that is the task of our highest courts and tribunals on both sides of the divide.

[70] *Jones v Ministry of the Interior of the Kingdom of Saudi Arabia* [2007] 1 AC 270; *Jones v United Kingdom* App nos 34356/06 and 40528/06 (ECtHR, 14 January 2014).

12

COMBAR: A Temple Bar Scholar's Perspective

KANNON K SHANMUGAM

Kannon was the guest speaker at the North American dinner in Seville in 2014. The al fresco dinner was held in the central courtyard of La Casa de Pilatos (Pilate's House), an Andalusian palace that is the permanent residence of the Duke of Medinaceli.

Kannon is a partner in the law firm of Williams & Connolly LLP in Washington DC. He leads the firm's Supreme Court and appellate litigation practice and has argued 17 cases before the United States Supreme Court. Kannon was a Temple Bar Scholar in 2000, a programme that COMBAR has sponsored for over 20 years.

I WAS DEEPLY honoured—but, I have to confess, more than a little surprised—when Stephen Moriarty asked me to contribute an essay to this volume to commemorate COMBAR's 25th anniversary. After all, in many respects, COMBAR is a quintessentially British institution—one might think of it as the legal equivalent of Wimbledon, the Proms, or Marmite. (Though, depending on your views of Marmite, you may wish to strike out the last.)

From its inception, however, a core part of COMBAR's mission has been to promote the virtues of the English legal system as a forum for resolving commercial disputes. Perhaps for that reason, while COMBAR may be an English Bar association, it has always been singularly outward-looking. And not surprisingly, the ties between COMBAR and the American legal system run deep. It is that aspect of COMBAR's work on which Stephen asked me to focus in my essay, and, in particular, on COMBAR's programmes for American lawyers. I am delighted to have this opportunity to reflect on my own experiences as a participant in those programmes.

As someone who likes to think of himself as still relatively young, I was astonished to realise that my first encounter with COMBAR came almost 15 years ago—back in COMBAR's infancy, or at least in its pre-teen years, when I was selected to serve as a Temple Bar Scholar. As most of the readers of this essay will be aware, the Temple Bar Scholarship was established in 1991 by the legendary Lord Denning and former United States Chief

Justice Warren Burger to strengthen the ties between leading members of the English and American Bars. Thanks largely to COMBAR, which from the outset has served as one of the programme's principal sponsors, the Temple Bar Scholarship now allows four or five young American lawyers annually to spend a month in London studying the English legal system up close.

I was privileged to serve as a Temple Bar Scholar in 2000, when I had recently finished a clerkship, or judicial assistantship, with Supreme Court Justice Antonin Scalia. Now, I have to admit that my motives in applying for the Temple Bar Scholarship were not entirely pure. I had a girlfriend living in London at the time, so the prospect of spending a month in London held a certain appeal. (I am pleased to report that the girlfriend in question is now my wife and the mother of our two wonderful sons, but that is a story for another day.)

Whatever my motives for applying, serving as a Temple Bar Scholar turned out to be a formative experience. I have previously described the Temple Bar Scholarship as the most important exchange programme between the world's two most influential legal systems, and it is hard for me to overstate what a remarkable educational experience it was for me. I was fortunate to receive an outstanding legal education at Harvard, our nation's finest law school. But I never took a class on the English legal system or on English legal history; in fact, I could probably count on one hand the number of times I had even read an English case. And my experience was hardly atypical. I suspect I was not alone among my fellow Temple Bar Scholars in thinking that the Master of the Rolls was the person who bakes the Queen's bread.

For me, then, the Temple Bar Scholarship was an opportunity to obtain a grounding in the English legal system—an opportunity that I never had in the course of my formal legal education. And thanks to COMBAR, I obtained that grounding by shadowing three of COMBAR's members—Ali Malek QC, then a newly minted silk, and Henry King and Rosalind Phelps, both of whom (like me) were just getting started in their careers at the Bar. (Perhaps my only disappointment was in learning that the real lives of young barristers were not quite as melodramatic as those of the barristers in *This Life*, which had just made its debut on American TV.)

I have to admit that I have only a dim recollection of the specific cases on which Ali, Henry, and Ros were working at the time. But I do know that, in that short month, we forged relationships that have continued to this day. Ali has been a mentor, as well as dear friend, throughout my legal career. And it has been a great pleasure to watch Henry and Ros as they progress in their own careers—and to trade notes, when we see each other, about the joys and occasional challenges of being a relatively junior lawyer in our respective countries.

One of the perks of serving as a Temple Bar Scholar is lifelong honorary membership in COMBAR—and, with it, the opportunity to attend COMBAR's annual North American meetings. I vividly remember sitting in my office in Washington, not long after passing the Bar, when Ali called me out of the blue to invite me to serve as a panelist at the 2002 meeting in Prague. At first, I dismissed the idea out of hand. But with Ali's typically irresistible advocacy, and thanks to the generous support of my law firm, I eventually agreed to go. And when I did, I was hooked.

I have participated in most of the North American meetings since, in breathtaking venues ranging from Istanbul to Vancouver. As anyone who has attended North American meetings can attest, they are wonderful opportunities to meet and renew acquaintances with leading commercial lawyers not only from Britain and the United States, but from Canada and a variety of other jurisdictions as well. But they are also opportunities to exchange views on major issues that simultaneously confront our respective jurisdictions—opportunities that, given the demands of modern legal practice, are all too rare.

I have many fond memories of North American meetings over the years, but perhaps my favourite involves the 2010 meeting, which was held in Lisbon. I was asked to participate in the moot, which at the time was the culminating event in the programme. That moot will perhaps best be remembered for Stephen Susman's cross-examination of Charles Béar, who was playing the part of an expert witness rather too expert at being a witness.

For my part, however, I remember the moot as one of the greater challenges of my legal career. For one thing, I was up against the formidable Catherine Gibaud, one of the finer advocates of my generation on your side of the Atlantic. For another thing, the topic was not exactly a neutral one—the question presented was whether European Council Regulation 44/2001 conferred jurisdiction over a declaratory judgment action brought against parties who were domiciled in the jurisdiction of suit. To put it mildly, this was not exactly a question on which Catherine and I were starting from the same point on the learning curve, European Council regulations having played a relatively small part in my practice before the United States Supreme Court. And for yet another thing, the moot was scheduled to begin at 10 am on Saturday—in other words, at 4 am Washington time. (As usual at COMBAR North American meetings, there was also a reception the night before at which the wine flowed freely, but I would like to think that both sides were operating at a similar disadvantage in that regard.)

I may not be the most experienced of advocates, but I know a stacked deck when I see one. And sure enough, I did lose, though not without a fight. At one point in the moot, I believe I described Catherine's arguments as being 'as solid as Greek sovereign debt'—which, with the benefit of hindsight, seems positively defamatory. To his credit, the presiding judge, Sir David Steel, seemingly recognised the need to level the playing field and did not subject me to the withering examination that my argument probably deserved. (Either that, or he too thought that a Saturday-morning moot on the interpretation of a European Council regulation constituted cruel and unusual punishment.)

All joking aside, it was an immensely rewarding experience to pit wits against a contemporary from another jurisdiction, on a substantial if alien question of law, and to observe first-hand the competing styles of advocacy from our respective jurisdictions. I suspect that few who were present for that moot remember very much about the comparative merits of our interpretations of European Council Regulation 44/2001. But I look back on that moot as a real highlight—apart from the result. (I am hopeful that COMBAR will restore the moot, so I can challenge Catherine to a winner-takes-all rematch.)

More broadly, I hope that my experiences with COMBAR, in their own small way, help to underscore why COMBAR's transatlantic ties are so important. The English and American legal systems do more than simply share a common heritage: as I said earlier, there can be no question that they are the two most influential, and important, legal systems in the world today. It is therefore vital that lawyers practising in each of those systems have a deeper understanding of the other. I am hard pressed to think of another organisation that has done more than COMBAR to promote an understanding of the English legal system among American lawyers. And I hope that, through programmes such as the Temple Bar Scholarship and the COMBAR North American meeting, the process has also worked in the opposite direction, as British judges and barristers have the opportunity, thanks to COMBAR, to interact with their American counterparts.

When I think of COMBAR, I think of an organisation that has the rare quality of being elite without being elitist. While the membership of COMBAR includes most if not all of London's leading commercial barristers, it is neither snobby nor exclusive. Instead, as I noted at the outset of this essay, it has always been singularly outward-looking: eager to tout the virtues of the English legal system, to be sure, but hungry to learn about other legal systems, too. That is not just a rare quality; it is a great one. I am confident that COMBAR will play an even more significant role in fostering transatlantic legal relations in the next 25 years than it has in its first 25. And I am privileged to join in congratulating COMBAR on this very special occasion.

www.ingramcontent.com/pod-product-compliance
Ingram Content Group UK Ltd.
Pitfield, Milton Keynes, MK11 3LW, UK
UKHW021906150926
475560UK00003B/216

9 781849 467056